Uncover the Truth

Uncover the Truth

Unlocking the Skills of Body Language and Statement Analysis

Sgt. Mike Ruggiero

Write My Wrongs Co, United States
www.writemywrongsediting.com

This book is dedicated to the fine men and women in this country and around the world who are committed to protecting and serving their community, city, county, state, and country. I had the honor of serving for more than thirty-four years with many amazing and dedicated people. Continue to fight the good fight. There are many more who support you than you know.

Table of Contents

Acknowledgments

I want to acknowledge my amazing family and thank my biggest supporter: my wife, Julie. Without her constant love and encouragement, I would not have been able to enjoy the career I have. I worked many long nights, missed a lot of dinners, and had to leave when the phone rang in the middle of the night. Not once did she complain or make me feel selfish. She has been and continues to be my better half.

To our wonderful children—Michael, Summer, and Alayna. They have all grown into adults who any parent would be proud of. I think I've learned more from them than they could have possibly learned from me. They have all been our blessing.

To the many people who have given me the opportunity to provide this type of training to first responders. Special thanks to Mark Waterfill and the great people at the Public Agency Training Council (PATC). Mark took a chance on me some years ago and I've had the honor and pleasure of providing my detecting deception training across the country.

Section I
Introduction

Well, they say everyone has at least one book in them. So what brought me to write it? After reading many books and attending in-person training on these topics, I found that all of them left me feeling somewhat unsatisfied, like there was much more that could have been taught or a lot that seemed overcomplicated. Although I've learned a great deal from what I've read, I'd like to offer information collected from books, training classes, and my own experience to help with the challenge of determining whether or not someone is being truthful. Of course, discerning the truth isn't something we have to do; sometimes, we'd just like to know if someone is being deceptive—for instance, a politician speaking about an issue, a coach at his press conference, or a person of interest in an investigation who provides a statement to the media.

I've been a law enforcement officer for more than thirty-four years. In addition to being on patrol and being the initial responder to incidents, I've had the opportunity to conduct numerous investigations regarding narcotics, persons crimes, sex crimes, internal affairs, and homicide. I've paid close attention during that time. In training classes I've taught, I like to say we work in our own laboratories. Here's what I mean: I didn't have to look very far to find examples to prove or disprove the ability to accurately determine truthfulness or deception. Does reality confirm them? Or does reality disprove them?

I've studied and taught the skills and techniques in this book for over twenty years. Just as importantly, I've applied them in numerous cases that weren't just my own but that were being investigated by my peers—in my own agency as well as throughout the country. I will provide specific examples, and you can draw your own conclusions. I believe these techniques work effectively, particularly for law enforcement officers. After all, someone's freedom may depend on whether or not an officer believes them.

However, these skills are also important for anyone who is in a field where finding the truth is crucial. They benefit private security personnel, lawyers, judges, HR representatives, teachers, and people who just want to learn about detecting others' deceit for in-person or digital interactions or even in media. Television today has many programs dedicated to profiling actual criminal cases. Many of them display the actual interviews that were conducted. Whether you're conducting your own interview or watching someone else's, these skills will prove valuable for you.

Let me explain a little about how I came to be an instructor of these topics. When I was a homicide detective many years ago, another detective in sex crimes came and talked to me about a case she was working. I'd had about ten years of investigative experience and was well-thought-of…at least, that was what I told myself! When she had explained her investigation, I stated that it sounded like she needed to write a search warrant. A search warrant involves providing an affidavit detailing what evidence you are seeking and where you expect to locate the evidence. The affidavit is then reviewed by a judge, who will sign it, authorizing the search. After talking a bit longer, she went back to her desk, only to return about ten minutes later. The detective asked me if I had a search warrant. Now, this wasn't a new detective; she had been in the Criminal Investigations Division (CID) for some time.

Indeed, she was investigating sex crimes, which is usually staffed with more experienced detectives. I gave her a copy of one of my search warrants to use as a template.

What concerned me was the lack of training that was available for our detectives. There was no formal training program in CID at that time. When a detective arrived in CID with their brand-new, shiny detective badge, they usually already had cases assigned to them. They were then told that if they needed anything to "get with someone." No training was available on "basic" skills needed by detectives: search warrants, arrest warrants, crime scene management, taking calls from patrol, responding to the scene as a detective, crime scene processing, triaging their caseload...you get the picture. It was basically sink or swim—and many sank.

Not long after the conversation with the sex crimes detective, I made a comment to my supervisor about the lack of preparation for new detectives and how the agency was leaving them unprepared. He said I made an interesting point—and then told me to put together some training. Well, I hadn't expected that and wasn't attempting to train anyone. But if not me, then who? If I wasn't willing to be part of the solution, wasn't I part of the problem? So, I began putting together materials for new detectives as well as those applying for an opening in our agency's CID.

What started as in-house training soon developed into a forty-hour course offered in advanced training locations. I called the class "Intro to CID," and it contained various topics useful to new investigators. For part of the curriculum, I taught short blocks on handwriting analysis and statement analysis. I had learned these skills and knew how effective they were, so I included them in the training.

Of course, a portion of the class was also devoted to interviews and interrogations. Most people don't realize that those going through the academy receive very little formal training on how to conduct effective interviews and interrogations. In fact, until about 2015, it wasn't even part of the academy curriculum in Florida. Once they've been hired as officers, they often go back to training centers to obtain advanced instruction on various topics like criminal law, field training officer, radar certification, defensive tactics, hostage negotiation, etc. An academy provides basic training, not the skills many officers will need as they continue their careers.

A few years after I had begun presenting the Intro to CID training, I was asked if I would be interested in leading the class on interviews and interrogations. Honestly, I had never anticipated being an instructor at all, let alone leading the prestigious Advanced Interviews and Interrogation class. After some thought, I decided to accept. I'd taken the class many years prior and thought I could offer some useful information. Although the class had a curriculum approved by the Florida Department of Law Enforcement, the instructor could add their own unique spin.

A short portion of the class was about kinesics, or body language. Since the class had to cover all aspects of interviews and interrogations, kinesics had to be a short unit. Although the class was technically Advanced Interviews and Interrogations, no prerequisite was offered, so I covered the basics of how to conduct effective interviews and the more complicated material for conducting successful interrogations.

Both of the classes had high attendance, and I worked hard to offer the best training possible. As I focused on not screwing up these great topics, I paid attention to the course evaluations completed by the students. It wasn't long before I saw a consistent pattern develop.

In Intro to CID, students wanted more information on handwriting and statement analysis. In the interviews and interrogations course, students wanted more information on the interpretation of body language. However, I had already packed the classes with material. I'm not the type to have a forty-hour class and bring about twenty hours' worth of instruction. Unfortunately, this is almost standard in many advanced law enforcement classes and can be a little frustrating, although not many people complain about two-hour lunches and finishing at three o'clock.

So my dilemma was how to teach more information without removing key concepts and gutting the classes entirely. Instead of switching material out, I decided to break those two topics away from the other classes and teach them as a separate course, a course I called Detecting Deception.

Detecting Deception covers the methods people use to deceive. I've noticed that it boils down to three categories: handwriting, body language, and statement analysis. At least one of these must be present for communication to exist. Now, you may have two of them, and you may have all three to analyze, but there must be at least one.

The more we know about the ways in which people are deceptive, the less of a chance someone has of "slipping one past us" because not everyone reacts the same way when under anxiety.

Disclaimers

Before we get any farther down this road, a few disclaimers. I don't present myself as having a PhD or being a chief. I rose all the way to the rank of sergeant and was quite happy there. Most officers will tell you that sergeant is about as high as you can go and still have your "boots on the ground." That was what I enjoyed: the challenge of working cases. My career goal was to become the homicide sergeant, and I was able to do that job for five years.

The fact is that I don't know many PhDs who have done a lot of interviews in a criminal setting. I also don't know many captains, majors, or chiefs who have conducted a lot of criminal interviews because they were busy getting promoted! I've read multiple books written by people with those qualifications, but unless you've investigated criminal activity and spoken to victims and witnesses, unless you've sat across from someone who has committed a crime they haven't yet been formally charged with—you cannot offer that perspective. That's what I've done for the last thirty-four years, and I hope you find the skills and techniques I've presented in this book useful.

The more someone has to lose, the more obvious their tells of deceit will be. That's because jeopardy causes tension, and tension causes the behavioral responses we look for. The stakes are high for law enforcement officers. We aren't talking about sending someone to bed early without dessert. We're potentially taking away someone's freedom.

For instance, consider someone who goes to a psychologist, a profession that obviously conducts a lot of interviews with various people. The difference between a psychologist and a law enforcement officer is that people don't have anything to gain by deceiving a psychologist. They're basically only lying to themselves. Similarly, a child who is deceptive with their parents may have minimal jeopardy attached to their deception. Understand that with little or no consequence attached to the deceit, the impact of stress will be lessened, which means the deceiver may not exhibit the signs of deception we're going to discuss in this book.

Now, let's get started!

Getting Started

In order to successfully detect whether people are being truthful or deceptive, we need some ground rules. My law enforcement brothers and sisters who have been doing this with varied success might need to unlearn some bad habits. First off, we must stop prejudging and/or forming opinions too quickly based on limited information. I'll tell you from the very beginning that the longer you wait to decide on whether someone is truthful or deceptive—the more information you have to analyze—the more accurate your judgment is likely to be.

As law enforcement officers, we tend to make quick judgments. However, when conducting an analysis, it's best not to judge too quickly. It's crucial that you conduct your evaluation without preconceived biases. It should come as no surprise that when people form opinions, they are unlikely to be swayed—even when presented with contrary evidence. You're likely to be hamstrung by what's known as "confirmation bias." Nobody likes to be proven wrong!

My advice? Analyze statements as fact. When people offer statements, they're communicating what they want us to know. It's a common mistake to "connect the dots" or to assume what the person *meant* to say or write. The statements stand on their own.

The more we learn about the human communication process, the more comfortable we'll be with the techniques involved in detecting deception.

You don't need to be a graphologist to see various signs in handwriting that offer insight toward the person's personality or signs of deception. You don't need to be an expert in neurolinguistics or micro expressions to effectively interpret someone's body language. And you don't need to have a PhD in English to utilize statement analysis. I've never been a fan of overcomplicating things; I prefer the "keep it simple" method.

Although I've also studied handwriting for many years now, this book will focus on body language and statement analysis. Experts can discern a great deal from handwriting, but there are some departments that are no longer taking written statements (which I believe is a bad idea), and a layperson reading this book is probably not going to be viewing many handwritten statements. In my class, I cover all three aspects of detecting deception. I decided to cover the more universal skills of body language and statement analysis. These separate but related skill sets better enable the recognition of truth and deceit.

While it's important to recognize when someone is being deceptive, it is just as important to recognize when someone is being truthful. It's a misconception that people lie to us. People may stretch the truth; they may be what I call "truthfully deceptive," and they may minimize something that occurred. However, most people don't fabricate events or details of events. It is far too difficult a task for most people to attempt to remember things that didn't really occur. As a result, they are more likely to simply omit details they don't want to admit while still maintaining the factual basis of their statement.

As a former law enforcement officer and someone who continues to offer training to many law enforcement officers around the country, I always ask whether it's important that we be able to recognize truthful versus deceptive behavior. And of course they agree because an arrest means someone losing their freedom. However, law enforcement officers also agree we receive little to no training in the skill sets that would prepare us to better detect deception. The result can be innocent people facing arrest for crimes they didn't commit, as well as guilty people going free.

I recall watching a real-crime TV program that featured a woman's interrogation. Two detectives were questioning her regarding her husband's homicide. Yes, we all know the spouse did it. Right? Well, this woman displayed two signs, one verbal and one non-verbal, that are consistent with truth telling. When I witnessed the behaviors, I made a mental note. Ten minutes later in the program, she was arrested and charged with the murder of her husband. I thought, *Maybe I misread the signs*? Thirty minutes later, the prosecutor had her released from prison after it was determined she'd had nothing to do with her husband's murder.

Now, I'm not saying that if someone displays truth-oriented behaviors that I'm going to end the interview and let them walk out the door. The detectives conducting the interview clearly believed she had been involved in killing her husband, or they wouldn't have made the arrest. In a case where there was no conclusive evidence of her guilt, deception-detecting skill sets were key.

I can name many, many cases where these skill sets put me on the right path, where the knowledge I've learned pointed me in the right direction. I'll use many cases I was personally involved in as examples in this book. In fact, I have a difficult time thinking of cases where these skill sets didn't apply or led me in the wrong direction. I rely on them to help me determine where to put my shovel down and dig.

After all, you're at a serious disadvantage if you don't have at least an idea of whether someone you are interacting with is being truthful or deceptive. By utilizing these techniques effectively, you can not only know *if* someone is being truthful or deceptive, but also *where* they are being deceptive. In addition, these skills may very well be the difference between closing a case and the case remaining open. You see, the problem isn't getting people to communicate with us—that is yet another misconception. The problem is interpreting the information we already have. The answer could very well already be in your case files.

There are also a few unexpected advantages about learning these skills. Yes, they can be applied to your current and future cases. But they can also be applied to cases we've already completed. The statements in the case file, the audio tape of the victim or witness interview, the video of the suspect in the case you worked two years ago…these skills can be applied to all of these examples.

We are going to be examining what is, to a great extent, simple human nature. As long as we are dealing with people, these skills will be beneficial. When I teach interview and interrogation classes (certainly a very important skill for law enforcement officers), the officer with the skills needs to be involved in conducting the interview for the skills to be beneficial. With these skills and techniques, you don't even need to be the person conducting the interview in order to conduct an effective evaluation regarding a subject's truthfulness or deception.

Before reading the book, I'd like you to ask yourself a question: how good do you think you are at determining whether someone is being truthful or deceptive? On a scale of zero to one hundred, where would you rate your ability? I'd like for you to take a minute and give it some thought. When you decide on a number, write that number in the margin here. At the conclusion of this book, we will revisit that number.

In his book *Telling Lies,* Dr. Paul Eckman details a study he conducted on the topic of deception. Some may know the name of Dr. Eckman; he is known as the "father of micro expressions" and was the basis of the popular show *Lie to Me*. Without delving into the details of the study, Dr. Eckman showed that people were able to discern the truthful person from the deceptive person 54 percent of the time. When participants only had two possible answers, 54 percent was only slightly over the odds of guessing correctly when there are only two options available. The fact is that most people are not very good at determining whether someone is being truthful for two reasons: first, because they follow misleading cues, and second, because they are unaware of other cues.

I base my training courses and this book on skills: talking to people, watching or listening to someone furnish an account of an incident, reading statements or transcripts of interviews, and interrogating people. Understand that for people to experience stress, which is the basis for deceptive behavior, there must be some jeopardy attached to their ability to convince others. Without jeopardy, there is no anxiety, and therefore, we may not observe the effects of anxiety through writing, body language, or the words they choose.

In this book, I will provide you with useful information you can utilize immediately. Though I will not go into great detail on the psychology, I will offer what I believe and have seen in the field to be the most effective aspects of these skills. Using the "keep it simple" method, I want to teach information that is useful and easy to understand, whether you are a homemaker or a homicide detective. This book will present skills you can utilize from the moment you read about them.

While each of these skills can take many years to become an expert in, they can still enable us to do our jobs effectively without investing years of learning. Or perhaps you just want "inside knowledge" on how to determine whether people are being truthful or deceptive. Whatever the reason, I hope you will find the material presented in this book both interesting and useful.

That being said, I advocate learning as an ongoing endeavor. I present these skills with the purpose of building a foundation. Readers who find them interesting and want to learn even more can build on that foundation in other ways. I have included resources in the bibliography to assist in doing just that.

I will be providing examples from many cases in which I was personally involved, as well as examples from cases the general public are already familiar with. Some of these cases caught national attention. We will apply the techniques taught in this book to those cases and then determine whether our conclusions match the truth.

Section II
Body Language

Lesson 1: Overview

I want to begin our venture into this section on body language, or kinesics, by establishing some ground rules. Here are some things it's important to remember as we learn:

- Remember these words: context, context, context! You must keep body language in the context of what the subject is discussing at that moment. The same exact body movements which may be a strong indicator of deception in one context might mean little to nothing in another.
- No one body movement insinuates deception in every situation. Remember: wait until you have as much information as possible before making a call on whether someone is being truthful or deceptive. One of my favorite sayings is "the more red flags we catch, the more certain we can be of deception." Body language is best read in what are known as "clusters"—or one movement

incorporating several smaller movements. For instance, someone leaning back in a chair *and* crossing their legs.

- We must consider the timing of all of the movements I'll discuss. People are going to move. They are going to shift in their seats. They're going to move their hands and feet. Not all movement means deception. We want to pay particular attention to the responses that occur within seven seconds of asking a question. Movement within that time frame is directly related to the tension a person is experiencing as a result of the question. We can therefore attribute those movements to the stress of deception.
- Last, a word we often hear concerning body language is "norming." Norming, or baselining, is the behavior a subject exhibits during normal conversation. If someone stutters, we can't count stuttering as a sign of deception. If someone has the sniffles, we can't count touching their nose as a sign of deception. That being said, we don't always have the luxury of norming a person's behavior. When we don't have a norm, we analyze their behavior based on what would be normal for someone in that situation—and how far from normal the behavior displayed was. Understand: courts do this on a regular basis. When it comes to the actions of individual officers, courts often base their decisions on what a "reasonable, prudent officer" would do. Essentially, they are using the "norm" as a measuring stick for the behavior of that particular officer. We can do the same thing when it comes to body language.

I recall an interview I was conducting with another detective. During it, I noted that this particular interviewee liked to talk. He didn't provide simple answers to simple questions. Now, most interviewers are trained to believe that not providing a simple answer to a simple question is a sign of deception. In this case, it was part of this subject's normal behavior. When we completed the interview, my colleague pointed out the subject's failure to offer simple responses and considered it to be deceptive. When I suggested that wasn't his norm—the interviewee did that with most every question—my colleague concurred.

I often ask my law enforcement students how they go about norming someone. I invariably get the same responses: ask them routine questions that are not about the case. Try to develop a rapport with them by asking some personal questions.

While this is a good start, we shouldn't stop there. Next time, try asking a few questions they have to think about to answer but have no reason to lie about. That will give you a baseline of the subject's behavior when they need to recall truthful information, and you can see whether they change from their norm later. Don't worry—it's not difficult. You can ask questions about their children's dates of birth, work address, their mother-in-law's address, etc. Anything that someone just can't snap out a response for will serve this purpose. Now you have a norm for what that person does when accessing factual information. This can be compared to their responses later in the interview. Their answers to these questions are unimportant; what I am paying attention to is what they *do* while they recall information with no motive for deception. Then I have a norm and will be able to see if they differ from it later in the interview.

Body language is the body's response to the anxiety caused by deception. In this way, the stress we are experiencing "leaks out" through body language. People who are being deceptive are usually exclusively focused on the words they are saying and not their own movements, which makes body language particularly telling. When non-verbal signs aren't congruent with a verbal message, we should zone in on their words because the probability of tension is high—and deception may very well be the cause of it. Let's look at some overall body language keys, then we'll talk about the body from head to foot.

Everyone experiences anxiety; some may do a better job of masking it than others, but everyone still deals with it. There are two types of responses to stress, which is why not everyone reacts in the same way: physiological and behavioral. Of course, it is the behavioral responses that are more closely associated with body language, and with good reason. However, it's important to have a quick discussion on the body's physiological response. As we'll see, physiological responses can manifest as behavioral reactions to the anxiety people experience when being deceptive.

Lesson 2: Physiological Signs of Stress

Physiological signs are the body's involuntary responses to stress. They are also commonly recognized as the fight-or-flight response—which is more accurately known as the fight, flight, or freeze response. Not everyone fights or flees. Some people simply freeze, but we'll get to that later.

Some common physiological responses include:

- Increased perspiration
- Changes in skin tone
- Dry mouth, dry lips
- Increased pulse
- Higher voice pitch

When faced with a tense situation, the human body automatically reverts to what is often referred to as "survival mode." People don't consciously choose this. I often use the example of a scene in the movie *Jaws*. In the scene where Richard Dreyfuss's character gets into the shark cage, he attempts to clear his mask using his saliva. Unable to spit, he looks up at Roy Schneider's character on the boat and says, "*I got no spit*."

This example shows that *stress* is causing the physiological response, not deception. Saliva is used for digestion. The body knows it doesn't need digestion in this moment; it needs oxygen for vital organs. Thus, the body is going into "survival mode." The body recognizes it doesn't need to produce saliva and diverts all resources to provide blood and oxygen flowing to the vital organs as it prepares for survival.

Another example of this is in Roger Clemens's famous interview, where he was asked about using performance-enhancing drugs as his former friend and personal trainer Brian McNamee had alleged. Although he had handpicked his interviewer and knew exactly what they would talk about, Clemens came off as a man under a great deal of duress. He had dry mouth during the interview and kept drinking from a water bottle. Clemens had dry mouth much like the previous example, but it wasn't because he was in a difficult environment. Clemens speaking to a reporter he knew well wouldn't account for the tension. The stress Clemens was experiencing was due to his need to be deceptive. This is why it's important to put our observations of body language in context of the given situation.

Not by coincidence, these are also the very same physiological responses measured by the devices many people commonly refer to as "lie detectors." The polygraph measures changes in heart rate, blood pressure, respiration, and perspiration through monitors attached to the subject's body. Much like I'm discussing in this book, the changes from the "norm," or baseline, indicate anxiety associated with deception in the context of the polygraph examination.

Another type of "lie detector" is known as the Voice Stress Analyzer, or VSA. The agency I worked with utilized the VSA for both pre-employment examinations as well as criminal investigations. I conducted many inspections as a VSA operator for several years. The technology behind it is rather simple. Again, when under duress, the vocal cords stretch and tense. This can be compared to the strings of a guitar. The tension causes more vibration when the person speaks and results in a slightly higher pitch. Now, the human ear cannot detect this subtle change, but the computer can. The VSA operator captures the subject's response, and that's what the computer graphs. The more vibration, the more stress associated with deception in the context of the examination.

However, there are times when you may recall someone responding to a question or just speaking, and their pitch becomes slightly higher. Again, in context, this is an indicator of some tension. Some time ago, I was in church and asked a friend how he enjoyed the holiday. He responded, "Oh, it was good," but I noticed his pitch was higher. Sensing that there was some anxiety that my friend associated with the holiday, I asked a follow-up question about how he'd spent his time. I quickly learned his in-laws had visited!

When I teach law enforcement personnel, another example I use is the "rookie" who gets involved in his first foot pursuit or car pursuit. We all recall how they sound on the radio when they call it in! Their pitch is a little higher, indicating they're under some stress. When one of the veteran officers calls in during a similar incident, supervisors often do a double-take and wonder...*Did he just call out he was in pursuit?* Their voice pitch usually doesn't change as much! So although it may be difficult for the human ear to detect, it's possible to hear a higher pitch when someone is speaking. Listen for any changes. If a "hot" question was just asked, and the change in pitch accompanies the response, it should be recognized as a red flag of deception.

***

Now, as I've mentioned, I worked as a homicide detective for ten years. There were times when I'd talk with someone and would notice the person sweating. In one particular case, I was speaking with a person of interest in a case, and his sweating—even though it wasn't warm out—led me to believe I was on the right track. This was an obvious sign of stress I think few of you would miss. His body was going into "survival mode," and that was the result. His words claimed he was not involved, but his body language was sending me quite a different message. He later confessed and was convicted of the homicide.

We'll later discuss some more examples of how these physiological responses can manifest in behavioral responses.

Lesson 3: Behavioral Signs of Stress

Behavioral signs are most commonly associated with stress and, at times, deception. They're the actions people use as coping mechanisms for the anxiety they're feeling. Sometimes, physiological signs develop into behavioral signs, and it's those signs that we associate with deception. We'll discuss some big-picture signs that people may display, then we'll get into more specifics.

Response Time

I'd like to start with a subject's verbal response to a question. Generally speaking, the longer a response takes, the less reliable its information. Response time is separate from statement analysis or the actual words the person uses. It's the timing versus the content of the response. When a question is asked, a truthful answer generally doesn't take a lot of thought. However, when someone is being deceptive, they need to think about how they want to formulate their response.

The subject may pause before answering to give themselves some time. The subject may ask to have the question repeated. They may repeat the question. All of these types of responses indicate tension. The question was a sensitive one, and the response should be carefully scrutinized.

Also pay attention to responses that seem rehearsed. I call these "locked and loaded" responses. Many times, law enforcement engages with people who know what it is we want to talk to them about, whether it's a burglary, sex crime, or homicide. Knowing this, the subject has often thought about how they are going to respond to questions. Hence their "locked and loaded" response; it isn't something they thought of in that moment. Subjects may also address a question that hasn't been asked yet. In those cases, the subject can't wait to be asked the question before spitting out their response—usually another indicator of stress.

A short video I use in my classes is of New York Representative Anthony Weiner addressing the media shortly after it was reported he had sent lewd pictures of himself to an underage girl. Certainly, Weiner was aware he was going to be asked about this. In addition, Weiner was a politician used to speaking to the media, and many politicians are trained by body language experts on how to best convey their message. Still, the signs exhibited by Weiner made it obvious he was under stress—and that was caused by his deception. Weiner was asked about the pictures sent from his Twitter account. He responded by attempting to use an analogy of "someone throwing a pie from the back of the room," and he wasn't going to let that be what he talked about. The reporters correctly pointed out that wasn't the situation and continued to ask him questions. Weiner's analogy only attempted to deflect from the issue and was an example of a "locked and loaded" response.

One of the points I make in my class is that Weiner didn't think of the analogy he used in the spur of the moment. It was clearly "locked and loaded." Weiner knew what he was going to be asked about and formulated the analogy in the hopes it would sidetrack the conversation. It didn't work with him, and you should be mindful when someone uses their "locked and loaded" story on you.

Response Pacing

Speech patterns are worth paying attention to. Fast speech is consistent with someone who is being truthful. The truth usually doesn't require a great deal of thought; therefore, the words can come quickly. This is also an indicator that the person isn't concerned with editing their responses as they would if they were being deceptive.

On the other hand, slow speech is an indicator of anxiety and possibly deception. The person needs to slow down their speech to be sure they don't include information they don't want you to know. Keep in mind, speech patterns need to be compared to the person's norm in order to properly gauge whether or not they are a sign of duress and possibly deception.

Body Positioning

How a person positions their body toward others can also be an indicator of stress. When a person is facing you, it's a good sign they trust you: they are being forthcoming. Someone who is being deceptive will often turn their body slightly away from you as a sign of their discomfort.

One good point of reference is the shoulders. If a shoulder is pointed toward you, the body is turned away. If this person is providing you with information while in this position, their intel should be carefully scrutinized. Generally, a person who is providing truthful information will be facing you and possibly leaning toward you.

Another good point of reference are the feet. A person's feet will naturally be pointed in the direction of what interests them most. If you observe a small gathering of people engaged in conversation, take a look at their feet. They will usually have them pointed in the direction of the person talking or whomever they find most interesting. If it is the exit to which the feet are pointing, they are interested in leaving the conversation. Law enforcement officers engage with people on a regular basis. If someone's feet are pointed in a different direction while speaking to you, it's a pretty good indicator they are contemplating going in that direction…sometimes very quickly!

Law enforcement officers are taught in the academy to turn our bodies slightly away from people we are engaging. This accomplishes a few things. First, it moves our firearms away from the person (the strong side is always the side away). Next, our vital organs aren't exposed to the person if they were to attack.

Even animals angle in a similar way, and they didn't need to attend the police academy! A dog will only expose its vital organs to someone it trusts. People are very similar in this respect. So if you're watching a surveillance video of an armed robbery at a convenience store, and the victim doesn't turn their body slightly away from the suspect…this is an indication of trust. There would not be trust with someone pointing a firearm—unless the suspect and victim know each other. In that case, you may be watching what is commonly referred to as an "inside job."

Posture

As stress affects the body, it often translates into poor posture. A person who is being deceptive will often have a difficult time sitting up straight. The upper body will begin to lean over their knees. I often refer to this position as the "pre-confession" position (it can also be called having "a monkey on their back"). The tension is taking a toll on them, with a feeling like there is a weight on their shoulders. For those of you who have done interrogations, this is a common body position to witness.

This body position doesn't usually occur in the first minutes of an interrogation. It takes some time for anxiety to have an impact on the posture, and people do have varying degrees of ability to deal with deception stress, but folding posture is far from uncommon. Often, it will be coupled with a downward, contemplative stare.

The person is now engaging in a mental bargaining. Should they confess?

An interviewer witnessing this body position can close the distance and even offer the person some comfort by placing a hand on their shoulder. Tell them you know how difficult this is but that you trust they will do the right thing. You know how this is weighing on them; telling you the truth will make them feel better.

Why do people tend to go into this position? When we are under great tension, we seek comfort. Even in adulthood, the fetal position remains a comforting position for us. This is very similar to the position described above. Many people may sleep in a variation of the fetal position. It is one of the ultimate positions of safety and comfort. That is also an explanation for why this position is cross-cultural: people of all backgrounds tend to assume this position when under stress. After all, we were all in the fetal position at one time.

Mirroring

"Mirroring" is another term commonly associated with body language. To "mirror" simply means to emulate the body position of the person you are engaging with in conversation. Generally speaking, people like others who are similar to themselves. So by assuming a position similar to that of the other person, you're conveying on a subconscious level that you're like them.

Now, if the person is in a negative position (their body is closed-off), you may not want to mirror them. Try assuming an open position while facing the other person, perhaps leaning forward slightly, and after a few minutes, the other person may begin to mirror your posture. People who relate to one another do this unintentionally.

Keep in mind that you can also mirror the language the person is using to achieve the same results. If someone uses a word, you then use that word back in your reply. However, mirroring of any kind should be done with subtlety. You don't want anyone to think you are mocking them, so if you're mirroring, it's best to wait a minute or so before taking a similar position.

An example of mirroring words can be found in the interrogation of O.J. Simpson conducted by the LAPD. Simpson stated he had "weird thoughts."

He said, "I've had weird thoughts…You know, when you've been with a person for seventeen years, you think everything."

Well, it doesn't take an expert in conducting interrogations to figure out what a pretty good question might have been: "What weird thoughts do you have, O.J.?" This would have been an effective way to verbally mirror the subject's words. Unfortunately, this wasn't done, and the interrogation in general wasn't effective.

While paying attention to a subject's body language is important, you must also pay attention to your own body language. Be careful not to exhibit negative body language, as this may cause the subject to unconsciously mirror you. Leaning back in your chair, crossing your arms, and crossing your legs are some examples of negative body language. Remember, the mind and the body are connected. A closed off or disinterested body points to a closed off or disinterested mind.

It's interesting to note that the concept of mirroring has been used to explain why people who have been together for a long time can start to resemble each other. By unconsciously mirroring each other and using the same facial muscles, over time, people can begin to look similar. In fact, this is also an explanation why dog owners sometimes resemble their pets!

Personal Space

If you're conducting interviews, you should have some knowledge of personal space and how it can have an impact on any discussion. In our culture, a space of about eighteen inches around us is considered our "personal zone." We usually only permit those close to us in this space. From eighteen inches to about three feet is the "friend zone." This is a distance for conversations with friends and acquaintances. From three feet to about twelve feet is the "social zone," where we can still interact with others but maintain distance. Beyond twelve feet is the "audience zone," which restricts personal interactions between a speaker and an audience.

Let's discuss the personal and the friend space because that's where most of our conversations occur. Entering someone's personal space can be an effective way to provide comfort and establish a connection or rapport. Note: this should only be done when appropriate. For instance, it would not be a good idea for an interviewer to touch a victim of a sexual assault or domestic battery. Likewise, it wouldn't be appropriate for a teacher to enter the personal space of a student. It's wise to follow the normal protocols of the given institution.

If you're engaged in a conversation with someone and they lean in closer to you, this is a strong sign of truthfulness. In fact, I previously mentioned a woman who was being interrogated regarding the murder of her husband. I said she did two things consistent with a truthful person when responding to a question—

one verbal and one non-verbal. This was the non-verbal response. She leaned in and closed the distance between her and the interrogators. It is very rare for someone who is being deceptive to move closer to their interviewer. This is true in personal conversations as well.

On the other hand, people sometimes may create more distance. This may be very subtle, so you must pay close attention. For instance, someone seated in a chair might lean back or lean away from the interviewer, or someone you're speaking with might move slightly away while talking. Again, this type of movement needs to be put in context. If someone is providing you with truthful, honest information, pay attention to whether they're closing distance or creating distance. If they create distance, it's likely something is making them uncomfortable.

The amount of space someone takes up also is significant. Someone trying to assert their dominance will take up more space. When you see a depiction of a superhero, they often take up plenty of space. For instance, they may place one or both hands on their hips.

Let's say your daughter is bringing over a young man for you to meet. You all sit down in the living room. Would you expect the young man to put his feet up on the coffee table? Maybe recline in the chair? Of course not! He'll likely take up little space because spreading out would be a sign of dominance or even arrogance. Now, after the young man is comfortable in his surroundings, he might take up more space because comfort and confidence go hand in hand.

Animals can offer an example as well. When an animal wants to portray that they are big and bad, they will make themselves larger. A cat's hair may stand up straight; a snake may raise its head to make itself appear more threatening. This is usually a warning to others to stay away. However, when preparing to attack, they tend to make themselves small. For example, a cat that is stalking its prey.

Now, when people are feeling contrite or hoping not to be noticed, it is common for them to assume less space. This was evident with the Boston bombing suspects as they made their way through the crowd. They took up little space in their attempt to go unnoticed. In addition, they didn't look in the direction of the explosion as they quickly left the area. This would also likely be the case with someone who walks into a store with the intent of shoplifting. Many people have cameras at the front door of their residences, and unfortunately, there are people who will follow around delivery trucks and relieve people of their packages soon after they are delivered. They are sometimes referred to as "porch pirates." Do you think these people take up little space or a lot of space? Yes, they will take up little space!

Many may recall the New Jersey Port Authority commissioner who inserted herself into a traffic stop where her daughter was a passenger in the vehicle. If you watch the video (which went viral), the commissioner assumes a position with her hand on her hip as she attempts to assert her authority. To their credit, the officers involved in the stop refused to be intimidated by the commissioner—they assumed the same position. As you remember, mirroring is often unintentional.

Of course, taking up too much space is perceived as arrogant, as it goes beyond conveying confidence and trips into overconfidence. For instance, a male sitting with his legs stretched out in front of him or with his knees far apart is sending a message of arrogance. The interviewer should pay attention to how much space the subject is taking up as well as whether the subject closes space or creates space when providing information.

Fight, Flight, or Freeze

The fight-or-flight response is well-known in many fields. It refers to the body's reaction while under great stress. However, while some people may fight and some may choose to flee, there is another reaction that goes unmentioned—the freeze reaction. You have probably noticed this response in your personal life, but it's also evident in television and movies. Usually, it happens when a character is so overwhelmed they cannot move their body. In the context of an interview or interrogation, we are more likely to encounter the freeze response than we are fight or flight. Even teachers or other authority figures are likely to see this response when having a disciplinary discussion with someone. As they are unable to flee or fight, their body may freeze.

There are a few explanations for this response. Of course, we've all heard of people who have become frozen with fear or been a "deer in the headlights," but I'd like to illustrate what "freezing" looks like in the context of an interview or interrogation.

In interviews where a subject is freezing, you may notice their body either isn't moving or has stopped moving at some point in the interview, even if they are able to speak with you and answer your questions. You see, moving the body while communicating with others is normal; it's natural. Not moving your body is not normal, so we have a break from the norm. When people are so focused on providing their story, keeping their facts straight, potentially anticipating questions, etc., they "forget" to move their body. Their energy is focused on their story, and the body may not move as it should when relaying an event in a truthful manner.

Well, the same thing can occur when a law enforcement officer or when any investigator or authority figure talks to people about something serious. This is unlikely to occur when speaking with a victim or witness to an event; it is usually associated with an interrogation or disciplinary-type discussion. The reason is the same as discussed above: during these types of discussions, the subject can become so overwhelmed that their body ceases any movement. Remember to analyze body movement in context.

Whether someone is in involved in a disciplinary discussion with an authority figure or a victim should inform your observations.

Now, this takes a good amount of energy and is a pretty certain sign the person is under significant stress. I've used the comparison of asking someone to hold a rubber band stretched out. It may be easy to do for five to ten minutes, but after twenty-five or even thirty minutes, it will bring the hands much closer together. Over time, it becomes more difficult for people to cope with the physical difficulty of maintaining their deception.

In my very first homicide investigation, I was conducting an interrogation with another detective. We were interrogating the wife of the victim, who had been brutally murdered. Our investigation had led us to believe the wife had conspired with her lover to kill her husband. I was the secondary interviewer, and my partner took the lead. He questioned her for approximately twenty-five minutes and used some very effective themes. As he questioned her, I noticed that her body had remained in the same position.

When he turned the questioning over to me, I pitched a scenario of what I believed had occurred. She looked at me and broke down crying. Her whole body went into the fetal position. My partner, who was seated closer to her, comforted her, and she soon confessed to her involvement in the murder.

Now, this wasn't because of my skills as an interviewer. You see, she had spent a great deal of energy maintaining the facade of innocence. The interrogation took nearly a half hour; it can be difficult for someone to maintain their composure for that long in that type of situation. After already spending so much energy, she suddenly wasn't able to keep the facade, and it came crashing down when I presented her with a probable scenario. The raw duress of an interrogation is likely to produce a freeze effect; bear that in mind when conducting these types of interviews.

Lesson 4: The Face

I want to discuss facial expressions in general before getting into more specific cues. The human face and body are symmetrical, and genuine expressions should appear symmetrical on someone's face and/or body. Sadness, happiness, surprise, among others, should encompass the face and appear balanced. Therefore, we should be paying attention to expressions which are not symmetrical. Often, they are not genuine, and they signal a disconnect between a person's verbal and non-verbal behavior. For instance, someone shrugs one shoulder when responding to a question in the negative. A smile that doesn't encompass the face. The asymmetrical expression of contempt flashing across the face of someone after a question is asked.

In research conducted by Dr. Paul Eckman, the facial expression of contempt was identified as being asymmetrical. We've all seen the look of contempt, where one corner of the mouth is turned slightly upward. I don't focus my training on what are known as "micro expressions" because I want to focus on expressions that can be identified in real time. I realize there are very few who will watch an interview on video and freeze-frame an expression that appeared for a fraction of a second. However, the look of contempt is certainly one that can be observed in real time. Watch for it, as it signals that the person is not pleased with a question posed.

For example, when the previously mentioned Representative Anthony Weiner was speaking to the media about his Twitter indiscretions, he flashed a look of contempt several times during the brief interview.

Here, New York Representative Anthony Weiner fields questions about a sexually inappropriate photo sent from his Twitter account to an underage female. Weiner flashes a look of contempt.

The Liar's Triangle

The Liar's Triangle is probably a term many of you have never heard. It refers to the area of the face just over the eyebrows, extending to the ears, then down to the chin. Interviewers should pay close attention to movement in this area, as it is closely associated with stress. Placed in the context of an interview or interrogation, the anxiety can often be associated with deception.

Eyebrows

Watch for an upward movement of the subject's eyebrows, which is often associated with someone who is seeking acceptance or is unsure of their position. It is also associated with other emotions (such as surprise), but I don't think many will confuse acceptance with surprise in the context of an interview or any discussion where someone is providing you with an explanation. For example, when athlete Marion Jones made her public denial of taking performance-enhancing drugs, she clearly raised her eyebrows and sought acceptance when she stated, "If the truth is told, then my name will be cleared, and I can move on with my life." Unfortunately for Jones, the truth was that she *was* using PEDs, to which she later admitted.

Eyes

You've probably heard that the eyes are the windows to the soul. That's because there is a lot of information we gather from eye contact, both consciously and unconsciously. The eyes are an integral part of interpreting communication with others.

I'd like to start by discussing eye contact. Pay attention to how much eye contact the interviewee is giving. Normal eye contact in our culture is about 30 to 60 percent of the time. Some people are led to believe that interviewees are supposed to maintain eye contact and any break in eye contact is a sign of untruthfulness—however, this isn't normal either.

In a study on deception conducted by Dr. Paul Eckman, when people were told to look directly at the interviewer while being deceptive, the ability of the interviewer to properly detect whether deception was present dropped to 35 percent for women and an astonishing 15 percent for men. Understand: there were only two options in the experiment—people were either truthful or deceptive. With a 50 percent margin of error, those numbers are really poor. The fact is that many people are aware that looking away might be interpreted as a sign of deceit and will look directly at the other person while lying. Don't be fooled by this.

When I teach my classes, I often tell officers to stop trying to "force" someone to confess to you while looking you in the eye. This is the hardest way to obtain a confession. As most of my students are law enforcement officers, I point out that many people are very happy to confess to the back of your head as you drive them to jail. I always see the more seasoned officers nodding their heads, as they have experienced this many times. People want to talk; don't make it more difficult. Make it easier. After all, making someone look you in the eye while telling you something that doesn't make them look very good is a difficult task.

I often use the example of a Catholic confessional. Most people are familiar with Catholic confessionals, or the private areas set aside for religious confessions. Does the priest come in and sit directly across from the person to take their confession? Of course not. There is a barrier between the priest and the confessor; a screen in the barrier makes it easier to speak while still not being able to see the other person.

Of course, many deceptive people will fail to reach the 30 percent threshold that is at the low end of what is considered normal eye contact. When engaging in conversation with someone, look for that 30 to 60 percent eye contact. Too much or too little eye contact should be considered a red flag of possible deception.

Paying attention to a lack of eye contact when someone is providing information is also important. If you take a look at the videos of Chris Watts (the man who murdered his pregnant wife and two daughters) in his initial contact with officers, you will see Watts avoid eye contact with the officer engaging him.

I would encourage you to base your judgment on more than just eye contact, but I would also advise you to avoid sitting directly across from the subject to make it easier for them to confess. Sitting in front of someone is more of a competitive position. We play board games and arm wrestle while sitting across from each other. Don't make an interview or interrogation a competition! Instead, make it cooperative, and consider sitting in a corner type of space or even beside the subject.

It's generally a good idea to go with the 30 to 60 percent that is considered normal eye contact in our culture. Extremes on either end—not hitting 30 percent or more than 60 percent—are worthy of attention.

In the documentary *Secrets of Body Language*, an experiment is conducted with two women sent to different car dealerships to determine the impact of salesmen on potential customers. However, the "customers" go to one dealership in the evening and the other during the daytime. While visiting during the day, the women were outfitted with sunglasses that had a built-in camera.

Any issues? Yeah, I have a few as well. First, sunglasses inhibit eye contact between the salesmen and the customers. In fact, the video "dings" the salesman during the day for failing to make eye contact with the sunglass-wearing customers. However, it's interesting that when the same women were interviewed by the body language expert, they put their sunglasses on their heads. Why? Because they wanted a connection with the body language expert.

It's a bad idea to wear sunglasses during any conversation where you're trying to establish a connection with another person. If it's so bright that sunglasses are necessary, it would be a good idea to wait until you can have the conversation at another location. Establishing a connection is essential in gaining truthful information in most any situation, particularly in conversations attempting to obtain an admission or confession.

Eye Movement

Studies have shown that right-handed people tend to move their eyes up and to the right when being creative (deceptive), up and to the left when accessing their memory, down and to the left when having an inner dialogue, and down and to the right when recalling something emotional. For left-handed people, the directions are flipped. For me, I've found it's easier to remember if I use an acronym. Law enforcement loves acronyms; we use them every chance we get.

Starting from the upper left as you are looking at the subject, the emotions are: Creative, Memory, Dialogue, Emotion—or CMDE. With those letters, I use Children May Decide Everything. If you guessed that my daughter was about ten years old when I was trying to think of an acronym, you are correct!

While this information is of value, it's equally important to norm someone to determine what it is they do when recalling factual information. Then watch for a change in the norm later in the interview when they ask a "hot" question. For a review on how to norm someone, please refer back to Lesson 1.

Did you know that studies have shown that people are more truthful to a computer than a human interviewer? When I mention that in my classes, there's some surprise. The only thing a computer can do that people can't is receive information with no emotional response. A computer cannot build a rapport; it cannot provide comfort or any moral justification for someone's actions. I believe a significant aspect of the study in question might have been interviewers who forced people to "look them in the eye" when providing a confession or some other embarrassing detail. We must refrain from judging those who admit their misdeeds. Fear of social condemnation can impede our ability to obtain honest confessions. I also believe this is another reason law enforcement agencies should be taking written statements. A piece of paper also offers no judgment.

Blinking

Pay attention to the subject's blink rate. A normal blink rate is about every four to five seconds, or twelve to fifteen times a minute. Someone who is under tension may blink at a much higher rate, which could mean the person is not confident in their message. Blinking is a good indicator because it's not something people tend to consciously control. Pay attention to a politician's blink rate when he or she gives a speech. If multiple candidates are engaged in a debate, the candidate who blinks the least is perceived as being more confident or in control. The people watching the debate won't be able to articulate *why* they find the lesser-blinking candidate more confident, but chances are they will.

Here is an experiment you can try. The next time you're watching a movie with a strong lead character (it could be a superhero movie, *James Bond*, *Mission Impossible*, etc.), pay attention to their blink rate when they're delivering a monologue. I'm willing to bet they won't blink much. They want to convey confidence.

I was watching *A Few Good Men* the other night. Jack Nicholson portrayed a colonel in charge of a base—needless to say, a powerful and confident man. When he testifies on the stand and gives his famous speech about ordering the "code red," he is almost completely unblinking. The same can be said for Tom Cruise's character, who questions him.

I recall watching the 1977 movie *Jesus of Nazareth* a few years ago. As I often do, I researched the movie while watching. I found that the director did not film the adult character of Jesus blinking once. Now, if I hadn't read that, I'm not certain if I would have picked up on that while watching, but if there is anyone who you would want to be confident in their message, I hope it would be Jesus!

So, if you are questioning someone regarding their involvement in an incident and they have a high blink rate, it may very well be because they are under considerable anxiety. Put in context of the interview, it's likely that deception is causing the anxiety.

Nose

People have a strong tendency to motion toward their noses when being deceptive. Some of this relates directly to the body's physiological response to stress, or the "fight, flight, or freeze" response discussed earlier. When a person is under anxiety and the body goes into survival mode, it sends blood to the vital organs. The nose fits into this category, as it provides oxygen; it also happens to have the thinnest membranes in the body, which means the sudden rush of blood to the nose will result in a tingling sensation—the person will want to itch their nose.

Keep in mind that this will be observable by many who are under duress in a variety of situations and is only a clue to deception when in the context of an interview or someone providing information. This is such a common clue to deception that there are many interviews where this is easily observable. Chris Watts can be seen going to his nose during his initial interview with detectives as well as Anthony Weiner during his interview with the media.

Mouth

The mouth is right in the middle of the Liar's Triangle. When under stress, people tend to move their hands toward it. It's almost as if they want to try to keep the words from coming out. Many of you can think of a time when one of your children said something they knew to be untrue and immediately put their hand in front of their mouth. As adults, people may try to disguise this natural reflex. Watch for anything that goes toward their mouth, such as a pen, glasses, even a drink. Movement toward the mouth offers people comfort.

Don't forget that when a baby is under duress, they may suck their thumb or be given a pacifier. Well, as adults, we still have this reflex. For instance, you might observe someone who is taking an exam place their pen on or in their mouth. Certainly, they may not be deceiving anyone, but they are still experiencing anxiety.

Ears/Hair/Head

Some people may realize that going to their nose or mouth may reveal the stress they are feeling. When their hands move toward their face, they may divert them to their ears or hair. This is still in the Liar's Triangle and worth noting if this movement occurs while they are providing information. In general, I've noted women tend to go toward their hair when experiencing tension more so than men.

When a male is engaged, you may notice his head is slightly tilted to one side. If this is coupled with an open body posture and perhaps a slight leaning forward or facing the interviewer, these are good signs of someone who is being forthcoming. Now, if the tilted head is being supported by a hand, it could signal boredom.

Women will tend to keep their head more vertical when engaged and paying attention. The more tilted her head, the more bored she may be.

Hands

After the face, the hands probably communicate the most and deserve the most attention. Hands can be symbols of comfort, control, authority, and power—and that can be without ever touching someone. Open hands are a universal sign of trust. Seeing someone's hands when they are speaking with you is a positive sign of open communication, whereas people who are being deceptive have the urge to hide their hands.

The arms may be folded to hide hands and hands may be placed behind the back, in pockets, or under the table. People have a natural tendency to want to hide their hands when uncomfortable; many people are uncomfortable when being deceptive.

Companies take advantage of our subconscious feelings toward hands as well. Think of the logos of Allstate and United Way. They both depict open hands because open hands are unconsciously associated with trust. At the same time, the palm of the hand is associated with submission, so an open palm or the "palm up" sign is an expression of such. The familiar "surrender" position is the ultimate submission symbol.

Bill Clinton during a debate showing the back of his hands to the audience. Politicians are often coached by body language experts to display positive body language signals.

Regarding palms, take a look at a couple holding hands while walking. The emotionally dominant person in the relationship will invariably be palm down. This may or may not be the person who is physically dominant. The submissive person will be palm up. This is an unconscious reaction to the relationship. Try holding someone's hand and reverse the position. Ask them how it feels. Almost invariably, they will feel uncomfortable in that reverse position. For instance, if I were to hold my wife's hand and put her in the dominant, palm-down position, she would be uncomfortable. However, if she were holding our daughter's hand, she would be comfortable in the dominant, palm-down position and uncomfortable in the submissive, palm-up position.

Touch

While we are on the hands, let's cover touch. Physical touch is an intimate thing and should be carefully considered because contact increases your influence and creates a positive connection. Politicians learn this early on. They will often touch someone they are shaking hands with on the shoulder or elbow for a brief two to three seconds.

An interviewer can provide comfort in a similar way if someone is feeling distraught during an interview. It shows we have genuine concern and empathy for them—and we should. Of course, it should be at an appropriate time and in an appropriate manner. With members of the opposite sex, it would be wise to refrain from touching them unless they reach out to touch you. In addition, using touch in an interview situation should be kept to only a few seconds. The effectiveness of using touch will not be diminished due to the short time frame.

If a subject does reach out and touch the interviewer during the conversation, this is an excellent sign of truthfulness. If closing distance is good, touch is even better. This is true in personal conversations as well as professional ones. Someone who is being deceptive generally won't touch the other person.

To illustrate the point further, Dr. Dan Ariely, professor of cognitive psychology at Duke University, conducted a study in which male and female servers touched the customers at some point during their service. Just a brief touch resulted in an increase in tips for male servers by 22 percent and female servers by 36 percent. Touch creates a positive impression on a subconscious level.

Lesson 5: Barriers

It almost goes without saying that barriers should be avoided when conducting interviews. Barriers can serve as just that in the communication process—they tend to hinder open communication. There are some barriers many are probably familiar with, and some are more subtle. Sometimes, we may not interpret things as barriers when we should recognize them as such. People may consciously or unconsciously utilize barriers when feeling uncomfortable or under stress. These objects can serve as barriers to open communication in general as well as to conceal specific body parts, so I'll examine both uses.

Objects as Barriers

People who are uncomfortable may subconsciously place an object between themselves and the person they are communicating with. Again, this is an indication of stress and does not always mean they are being deceptive. For instance, when my wife and I are enjoying dinner together at a restaurant, I sometimes observe couples seated at other tables. You have probably noticed that most couples prefer to sit across from each other. If they are seated across the table, sometimes they'll place their beverages between them, which indicates they may be somewhat uncomfortable.

Now you may be thinking, *Wait, I thought you said we shouldn't sit across from someone because it's a competitive position.* You are correct—in an interrogation setting. In the case of a restaurant date, we're considering two people who probably want to maintain *more than* that 60 percent eye contact! In nonconfrontational settings, any eye contact above 60 percent means the person in question is probably more interested in the speaker themselves than what they're talking about. This is the reason why couples often sit across from each other: so they can get more eye contact and build a connection with the other person.

In other environments, a barrier could also be a folder that someone is holding or placing between themselves and the person they're communicating with. Children may hold a stuffed animal or favorite toy during an interview. You must be careful, as these objects may serve as barriers to open communication.

Chairs as Barriers

Keep a few things in mind if you use a chair during an interview. First, I'd suggest the interviewer's chair to be nicer than that of the subject. I want interviewers to be comfortable, as some interviews may be lengthy. Nicer chairs also create the image that interviewers are important. When you go to the office of your supervisor, he or she is in a nicer chair, and you have a lesser chair on the other side of the desk. Can you think of a situation where the person in control or on their "home field" doesn't have a nicer chair? Note: there are some situations where the chairs and/or table are designed to provide all with equality rather than tacitly promote a hierarchy. For instance, a round table promotes equality of those seated and it would be unusual for someone to have a higher or nicer chair.

The chair should also be height adjustable to maintain a position of dominance. You don't want a situation where the interviewer is forced to look up to the person they are interviewing because it would forfeit a position of dominance to the subject and should therefore be avoided. I sometimes use the example of a courtroom to demonstrate how chair height is akin to authority. The lowest chairs in a courtroom are those in the gallery. Next are the chairs where the defense and prosecution sit. Next are the chairs of the jury. The witness testifying is normally seated a little higher, and the judge is seated the highest.

Both chairs should also have arms. I want the subject to be able to rest his hands on the arms of the chair to discourage him from folding his arms in front of him. A chair's arms also keep a subject from turning their chair around and sitting backward, preventing them from using their chair as an effective barrier.

As the sergeant in homicide, I recall watching two of my detectives conducting an interrogation of a person of interest. They were excellent interviewers, and the interview was already in progress. When I tuned in to monitor their interview, I observed the subject seated backward in an armless chair as described above. I was fairly certain they weren't going to be successful. Later that day, one of them asked me if I had seen the interview. I said I had and asked if it had been effective.

My detective said it hadn't been, and I asked why he had permitted the subject to sit with the back of the chair between him and the interviewer. He knew where I was going with my question and said he'd been seated that way when the detectives had entered the room. The back of the chair had provided the subject with a useful barrier to keep the detectives from getting too close and gave him added security, similar to someone behind a podium. While I'm not saying someone sitting in this manner makes it impossible to obtain a confession or admissions, it will be quite a bit more difficult. In fact, I have a difficult time thinking of an instance where someone sitting in that position *did* confess. In hindsight, it would have been a good idea to have the officers ask the subject to turn around in his chair before starting the interview.

Let me attempt to clarify the difference between an interrogation and a custodial interview. An interrogation can be conducted anywhere, and custody is not necessary. An interrogation can be conducted anywhere by anyone—from mom trying to find out who broke the lamp to a police detective questioning a homicide suspect! I've obtained many confessions at locations other than a police department. A custodial interview means the person has already been criminally charged and is in police custody.

While we are on the topic of custodial interviews, I'd like to mention a quick piece of advice to my law enforcement readers. Many detectives conduct these with people they have charged with a crime. As a routine and if possible, I would suggest that the interviewer be the one to un-handcuff the subject. This accomplishes a few things.

First, it suggests, without saying a word, that the interviewer controls the subject's freedom. They have the authority to take off the handcuffs. Next, because it frees the hands, the officer can observe their body language more easily. Last, it leaves no doubt as to who is in control of the interview.

Keeping the handcuffs on will only serve as a constant reminder that they are going to jail. Of course, always be mindful of officer safety when doing this. Although the subject should have already been thoroughly searched, you can always conduct another search. Consideration should also be given if the person is a flight risk or if there are only one or two officers in the area where the interview is being conducted.

For my readers in the private sector who don't need to concern themselves with the idea of custody, I would suggest interviews like these be conducted at a neutral setting rather than the interviewer's office. Conducting interviews at the office of the interviewer usually presents many distractions and could provide the interviewee with the opportunity to control the interview.

Many times, the person being interviewed would be an employee. I would also suggest having the interviewee give a statement as to their knowledge of the incident or complete a questionnaire specific to the issue under investigation prior to conducting an interview. Leave the subject alone in the room to complete the statement/questionnaire. As we will later see when we discuss statement analysis, this will help identify areas that require further questioning.

Once the statement/questionnaire is completed, have the subject wait in the room while you quickly evaluate the information in their statement. Much the same as the previous law enforcement example, doing this establishes the interviewer is in charge of the contact.

For seating, I would recommend a nicer, higher chair for the interviewer. Consider sitting on the same side of the table or a corner position from the interviewee.

Arms as Barriers

Of course arms are commonly associated with barriers. A person's crossed arms are a sign that they are not open to communication. To remove the barrier, you could ask them to give you something, such as their identification, or offer them a beverage—anything that would force them to uncross their arms and open their posture. This is another reason why chairs with arms are good for interrogations, as previously noted.

I recall working a detail with a friend of mine. As we were standing together, a woman approached us from his side and walked past him to ask me for directions. After I provided them, he asked why she had passed by him to engage me. I pointed out he'd had his arms crossed, sending a signal that he hadn't wished to engage. I'd had an open posture when she'd approached. People react to the body language signals we send.

Legs as Barriers

Right along with crossed arms are crossed legs, which also create a barrier. Some may even put a hand on their lower crossed leg in order to brace themselves. This is a withholding position that stems from anxiety. In addition, note that one foot will obviously be off the floor in this position, so if someone who is allegedly confessing or providing you with forthcoming information sits like this, their information should be carefully considered.

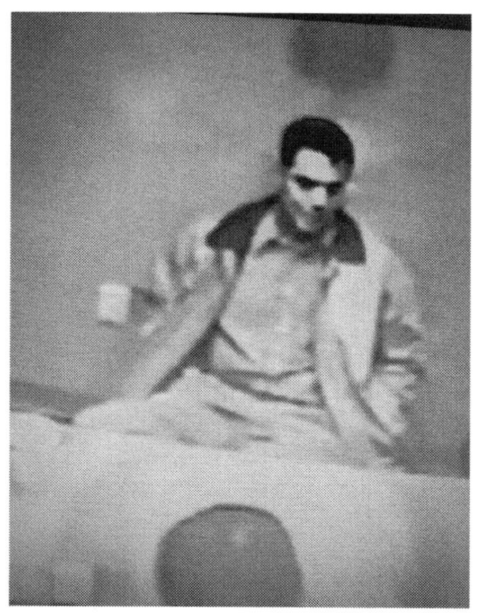

Here is a still photo of Scott Peterson during his initial statement to police regarding his missing wife, Laci. Note how he is leaned back, hands in his pockets, and legs crossed. Is this normal behavior for a man worried about his missing pregnant wife?

When it comes to seated males, the closer their knees are, the less confident they are. A man sitting with his knees close together is sending the message that he is feeling somewhat vulnerable. Of course, we should always pay attention to the opposite extreme: someone sitting with their knees spread wide is sending a message of arrogance or cockiness.

Here, President Roosevelt is pictured with Stalin and Churchill. Notice how close together Churchill's knees are. Both Churchill and Stalin are also covering their genital area. These body positions, with men in particular, indicate a feeling of vulnerability.

If a man is covering his privates, whether seated or standing, this is also a strong indicator that he doesn't feel confident. A man may try to disguise this by placing an object such as a hat or paperwork over his lap, but the message is the same.

In the previously mentioned infamous interview with Representative Weiner, he was standing with his hands covering his privates. This was a strong indicator of how vulnerable and defensive he was feeling. He didn't consciously think about his vulnerability and decide to take that position. The mind and the body are connected, and the body often projects our emotions.

In the famous photo of FDR, Winston Churchill, and Joseph Stalin (taken at the Yalta conference after World War II), their body language tells a story. FDR is seated in the middle and appears to be the most dominant figure. Why? Churchill is sitting with his knees close together and is covering his lap with his hat. Stalin is seated, and although his knees are slightly farther apart, his hands are folded in his lap. FDR's knees are spread—not so far as to indicate cockiness, but rather an assured dominance.

On an unrelated note, there is something else few people would notice. FDR is wearing the lightest clothing of the three. It is a misconception that heavy clothing makes one appear more dominant. It actually has the reverse effect. Large, heavy clothing diminishes the wearer. In this case, Churchill is wearing a heavy coat, and it makes him appear like a turtle peeking out of his shell. It has a diminishing effect on projecting authority.

Feet

There is an old saying that goes, "When people make a big decision, they do so with both feet planted on the floor." If you're in law enforcement, I urge you to take a look at interviews you've conducted or observed; if you're in a different profession, I'd encourage you to pay attention the next time you have a sensitive conversation with someone. Are their feet on the ground? When someone is providing a confession or making an emphatic declaration (of their innocence, for example), you will invariably find that their feet are on the ground. The nervousness caused by deception stress causes them to want to lift their feet—one or both—off the floor.

I can't tell you how many times I've observed this play out. One of the interviews I show my classes is one a *New York Times* reporter conducted with Jerry Sandusky after he had been arrested and charged with forty counts of sexual battery. During the interview, Sandusky is never shown with both feet on the floor. It's very subtle, and unless it's something you pay attention to, you wouldn't notice it.

I was watching an interview on a real-crime program of a woman whose husband had been the victim of a homicide. It was the California case of Angelina Rodriguez. It turned out that he had been poisoned, and early in the investigation, detectives were interviewing Rodriguez, who was providing information to assist in the investigation. During her interview, Rodriguez never appeared to have both feet on the floor. While watching, I told my wife, "She's probably involved." Again, there was a disconnect between the verbal and non-verbal behavior I witnessed. When that's the case, it's a good idea to rely on the non-verbal communication. If you watch clips of Jodi Arias's interview with police, as well as the interview with a then nine-year-old Burke Ramsey after his sister JonBenet was found dead, you will also see them pull both feet off the floor.

Now, I don't want anyone to get the impression that I would conclude that these people are guilty based upon just a few gestures. They are indicators, red flags of concern. The more red flags I detect, the more certain I am of deception—and you can be as well. These observations cause me to dig deeper, ask more questions. Questions like, "Tell me more about…" or "Who else did you see that day?" These questions invite the interviewee to fill in information they have previously left out. They also may believe the interviewer already knows the answer.

However, these skills should be used in conjunction with a thorough investigation, not in place of one. You see, when you ask good follow-up questions, you then force the person to either lie to you or be honest. This makes deceit much more difficult for them, and you will then have either a confirmation of deceptive body language (if there are additional signs of deception observed), or the person will convince you that they are being truthful.

Self-Comfort

Look for signs that the subject is providing self-comfort as a relief for stress. The most common form of this is rubbing hands or fingers together. They may put their hands behind their back when doing this. Some may rub their arms, temples, or even legs if in a seated position. This is a sign they are feeling some tension, and the tension may be linked to deception.

Another sign of self-comfort is when someone folds their arms so tightly that they appear to be giving themselves a hug. They are providing themselves with reassurance and saying to themselves, "I can get through this." Note how the palms are turning toward the body to provide comfort. While not necessarily a sign of deception, it is certainly a sign of anxiety, and (taken in context) it could be an indicator of deception.

In this still photo taken from a police body camera, Chris Watts gives himself self-comfort as he interacts with the first detectives on-scene investigating his missing wife and children.

Gestures

These signs may be more difficult to spot, but they are good signs of stress. Look for gestures that are out of sync with what the person is saying, for someone who motions in one direction while speaking in another. It's out of sync and therefore a sign they are under duress. In fact, this is difficult to do unless you think about it. However, these people *aren't* thinking about it—they do it because they are under stress and it is causing their gestures to be out of sync. Need an example? Take a look at former President Clinton's denial of having sexual relations with Monica Lewinski. Yep, it's there. Clinton looks to his left and gestures to his right.

Of course, Bill Clinton is a master of using body language to his advantage. It was a big part of his charisma. In early Clinton speeches, he tended to gesture with his hands away from his body. It's probable, though not certain, that Clinton might have been coached by a body language expert when he started appearing on the national stage. As Clinton became more polished, his gestures stayed closer to his body. His hands remained between his shoulders and his waist. In political circles, this is known as "The Clinton Box." These are power gestures.

You see, gesturing far away from your body is perceived as emotional. Now, emotional is fine if you're a college coach, but it's not so fine for our political leaders. It can lead people to believe you might react emotionally in situations that require clear, calm logic. Think of people you know who tend to gesture away from their body, and you will probably agree.

Another example of an out-of-sync gesture is when someone responds to a question with a shrug of one shoulder. This is incongruent. For instance, you ask someone if they have seen their neighbor, and they shrug one shoulder. Most people will shrug both shoulders when providing the "I don't know" response.

This is a photo of Jerry Sandusky as he answered questions from a reporter regarding sexual abuse allegations. You can see Sandusky gesturing in one direction while speaking in another.

Time

The impact of time is often disregarded by most law enforcement as well as people in general. As we've discussed, stress can have a debilitating effect on someone. The effects of tension can put someone in the hospital, so it should not be minimized. Someone who is speaking with law enforcement or any authority figure regarding a specific issue is under considerable duress, particularly if they are or are going to be deceptive. I'd like to discuss the impact of time and how we can use it to our advantage. Don't make it easy for people to be deceptive with you!

If someone is coming in for an interview, I suggest that you let them wait in the lobby for a few minutes. Understand that if they are going to be deceptive with you, they have set their internal clock, and they are going to lie to you at a given time. The body is going to "gear up" for the anxiety of deception and enter the fight, flight, or freeze mode we previously discussed. This, in turn, will increase their level of stress and make their body language clues easier to read. It also makes clear who is in control of the interview, and that's not a bad thing.

If you can ask someone else to escort them to the interview room, all the better. Maybe even monitor their behavior while they wait for a few minutes. Before you begin your interview, look for extremes: someone who puts their head down to fall asleep or someone who can't sit still.

Generally speaking, the longer the interview goes, the harder it will be for someone who is being deceptive to maintain the facade. Now, I'm not advocating for marathon interviews. In fact, if the interview is approaching two hours, it's best to take a break. Get a beverage, let them use the restroom, or even offer them something to eat. Continuing to question someone beyond two hours may elicit an untruthful comment from an honest subject who just wants to end the interrogation. My experience has led me to conclude that most false confessions occur after the two-hour mark. My point is that if your interrogations are going for fifteen to twenty minutes before you either run out of things to say or they devolve into a verbal tug-of-war, you may not get many confessions or admissions.

It has been my experience that most successful interviews are between about twenty minutes and two hours. If the interview lasts twenty minutes or less, the subject is able to maintain their facade; they can metaphorically hold up the wall and keep from verbalizing an admission or confession. The effects of stress on those who are being deceptive will not have overtaken them. However, going beyond two hours can take a mental and physical toll even on those being truthful and cause them to tell the interviewer(s) what they want to hear in order to end the interview.

This dynamic also works in the sales field. It's why you sit through a presentation for the timeshare sale; it's why car dealerships all have cafés in them and will appraise and purchase your car, even if you don't buy a car from them. There are even cafés in furniture stores now. This is all designed to keep you at the location for additional time. They know the longer you're there, the better the chances are that you'll make a purchase.

I was furniture shopping with my wife at a large furniture store in town. It had been years since I'd been in a furniture store and was surprised to see the café. They had drinks and were even baking fresh cookies! Well, I would have to wait another ten minutes for the next batch of cookies to come out, so I suggested we take another look at the bedroom set. Yep…that free cookie set me back $2,500!

Conclusion

While it is always safe to say that no one sign is a definitive indicator of deception, it's important to reiterate that we must always pay attention to the timing and duration of signs. You may see one particular sign for an extended period of time. For instance, during the interviews with Jerry Sandusky and Angelina Rodriguez, they did not have both feet on the ground for extended periods of time.

While this detail still only amounts to one sign, its significance is increased by its duration. Wouldn't it be a significant sign if someone kept their hand in front of their mouth during most of an interview? There may be instances where you see a sign repeated often—excessive eye blinking would be another example—that increases the likelihood that the person is being deceptive.

Many police departments as well as the various civilian organizations tasked with conducting an investigation utilize two interviewers to conduct crucial interviews, and it's not unusual for several to be at the initial scene of an investigation. It's important to remember that when you are not the primary interviewer or investigator, you have even more opportunity to observe the body language of those around you. The lead interviewer or investigator on a case is often the one conducting many of the interviews. Their attention is focused on their line of questioning, evidence, what other witnesses said, etc. It can be very difficult to monitor the non-verbal signs accompanying the verbal responses along with everything else. As a secondary, your plate isn't as full, and that allows you the benefit of paying additional attention to body language.

Students have often asked me whether they should tell someone when they're noticing their body language. I don't give a definitive yes or no. If you think it will further your interview, then sure. But I wouldn't mention it unless I was certain it would help the interview. Remember that your comment will alert them to you paying attention to their body language. Do I point out behavior on a regular basis? No, but there are times when I have.

Some time ago, I was conducting an interrogation of a young man in Parkland Hospital who had sustained severe burns while committing arson to cover up a homicide (he wouldn't be the first; this is not uncommon). I was about fifteen minutes into the interview when I'd noticed he'd begun staring at the ceiling for an extended period of time.

He was lying on the bed and looking up, but his expression was a blank stare. He was no longer making eye contact with me. What was he doing? He was mentally leaving the interview. He was wishing he was anywhere else at that moment—and, in all likelihood, that I was somewhere else as well. As long as he was in that state, I wouldn't be successful with my questions. So I told him that I knew what he was doing. I told him I knew he was attempting to mentally leave the interview, but that I wasn't going anywhere, that he needed to come back so we could talk about it. He did. And a few minutes later, he confessed to what he had done.

I thought my pointing out the behavior would work to my advantage. He then thought I even knew what he was thinking—and that was what I wanted him to think. However, this is more the exception than the rule. Generally, I don't go around pointing out my observations regarding body language. In social situations, it would only serve to make people uncomfortable and probably self-conscious. In an interview situation, more often than not, I prefer to use the information to know if I'm on the right track. A detail I didn't mention in the story I related was that time wasn't on my side in this particular interview. I was in a hospital and was informed the nurse would be taking him for further medical procedures. As I wasn't sure exactly when that was going to occur, I wanted to make the most of the time I did have.

My point is to utilize these skills to conduct a more thorough and complete interview and investigation. Use the skills to provide you with guidance on whether you're on the right path. After all, if you don't know where to put your shovel and dig, you are on a fishing expedition. These skills offer insight into which questions or topics are sensitive or making the subject uncomfortable. Try to deduce these topics, then continue to focus your questioning in those sensitive areas. Are the non-verbal responses consistent with the verbal responses? If they are, it's a good sign that the person is being honest and forthcoming. If not, perhaps it's time to dig.

Section III
Statement Analysis

Introduction

As I've stated, I teach foundational skills in handwriting, body language, and statement analysis in my detecting deception class. I frequently remind students that I will provide them with enough information to implement the skills immediately, but there is far more to be learned than what I teach. I've studied these skills for more than twenty years now, and I can't convey everything in a class that lasts only a few days. I encourage them to continue to learn, practice, and develop these abilities.

However, if someone told me I could only use *one* of these, I would choose statement analysis. It's powerful because it has the widest application. Amazingly, many in law enforcement have failed to take advantage of the benefits it can offer. The knowledge gained from conducting a statement analysis can be the difference between a case that remains open and a closed case.

To illustrate this point further, in 2016, the FBI completed a comprehensive evaluation of homicide investigations conducted across the country. Annually, all law enforcement agencies report their crime statistics to the FBI for inclusion in the Uniform Crime Report they compile. Many are not aware the average clearance rate (clearance means the case has been solved) for homicides across the US usually hovers between an average of 60 to 65 percent. Translated, this means on average across the US, about 60 to 65 percent of homicides are solved. Well, the FBI looked into why some departments had higher clearance rates than others. Many factors were considered in the study, from how detectives were selected for the assignment to the organization of case files.

One of the factors considered was the use of statement analysis in conducting these often difficult and complex investigations. Unfortunately, only 16.4 percent of departments reported using statement analysis. However, when that was the only factor taken into consideration, the FBI found that departments who reported utilizing statement analysis also documented an average clearance rate 5.2 percent higher than the departments that didn't utilize statement analysis.

This figure is as shocking as it is disturbing. Why wouldn't departments use a tool that could help them clear not just homicides but all types of investigations? Because if it's not being utilized in homicide investigations, it probably isn't being utilized in the investigation of other crimes either.

It's confounding. Agencies and individual detectives should constantly strive to enhance their skills. We should be seeking tools that can assist in conducting more thorough investigations. But despite advances in DNA analysis, the ability to track the cell phones being carried by almost everyone, and the near-constant presence of surveillance cameras, the clearance rates for homicide have *gone down*. In 1980, the UCR clearance rate was 72 percent! So these advances have not translated into higher clearance rates. If utilizing statement analysis will make over a 5 percent impact, it would no doubt have a similar impact on other crimes as well.

The result is hundreds of unsolved cases due to a lack of training in this one area. It also lends credence to something I mention during my classes—the answer to the case likely already lies in your case files. It is yet another misconception that people don't want to talk to the police. They do want to talk; the problem is that many law enforcement officers don't know how to properly evaluate the information they already have. In fact, I will offer some very specific examples of this breakdown in coming pages.

One of the many positive features of statement analysis is that its uses are not restricted to only a few people in the department. Everyone from the patrol officer to the homicide detective can use the skills in statement analysis. I will give examples from numerous cases, many of which came across my desk. Not just law enforcement officers, but private investigators, security, lawyers, school administrators—anyone who wants to obtain the truth.

Communication that can be analyzed using statement analysis:

- Victim
- Witness
- Suspect
- Complainant
- 911 calls
- Transcripts of audiotaped statements
- Videotaped interviews

The analysis requires only the words used by the subject. Now, unlike learning aspects of body language, many in law enforcement have developed habits that can have an impact on their ability to conduct this effectively. So I'd like to start there.

Collecting Statements

Taking written statements is not a regular practice across all US law enforcement agencies. In the department where I worked, we took statements on almost every initial investigation conducted by patrol officers. Those statements would then be forwarded to Criminal Investigations. If your department is not taking written statements, I urge you to reconsider. They pose no risk to the investigation, and the benefits are many:

- You now have sworn testimony directly from the person.
- You have an account of the event in their own words.
- When detectives arrive, they can quickly review pertinent information provided by those at the scene.
- Easy reference for detectives. I can tell you from experience that most detectives rarely listen to any of the audiotaped interviews they conduct. Conversely, it is quick and easy to refer back to a written statement.
- Prosecutors have a sworn document in order to facilitate the filing of criminal charges.

Remember that you always have the ability to collect a supplemental audio or video recorded statement. As a detective for more than twenty years, I can tell you I have reread far more written statements than I have re-listened to audio-recorded statements (which must be transcribed if you want to read them). There is simply no downside—and I haven't yet gone into the many clues a competent statement analysis can produce.

Patrol personnel can be easily trained to separate witnesses from other people and give them a written statement form. The importance of separating people cannot be overstated. Failing to separate the person providing the statement could lead to the information being tainted by outside individuals. This is true for any investigation, not just those conducted by law enforcement. The form should have all necessary information for the witness at the top of the page (name, address, phone, email, etc.). The person can then provide information they choose about the incident.

When obtaining a statement, it's important not to direct the person what to write down, where to begin, and what to include. Only one sentence is necessary when giving the statement form: "Please tell me what happened, and provide as much detail as possible."

If the person asks, "Where do I start?" Tell them to start from the beginning. No additional directions should be necessary. If it's important for specific elements of the crime to be clearly stated, or if you would like them to include the value of lost/damaged/stolen items, have them skip a few lines and include that information below. That information is not needed for the analysis. Written responses like this are known as an open statement. In other words, they haven't been influenced by anyone.

Misconceptions About Deception

It's a misunderstanding that people don't want to communicate information to others. We have a basic need to communicate with others and, further, to be understood by others. The problem isn't getting information as much as it is *interpreting* information we already have. Sometimes we're so busy trying to find the lies that we are missing what is actually being written or stated.

The next misconception would be that everyone lies. In my experience, most people don't lie in open statements; instead, they simply don't provide information that might incriminate them or make them look bad. It takes considerably more effort to invent a lie, so most people don't. Lying is relaying an idea that has no basis in fact or truth. It's difficult because there is no real memory of the lie. That means it's also difficult to recall the same lie at a later time. More often than not, people simply omit the information they don't want you to know.

The third misconception is that victims and witnesses are telling us the truth and suspects are lying. Anyone who has conducted investigations knows this is hardly the case. If a preconceived notion is formed that the person is going to be truthful or deceptive, you have already set yourself up for failure. In order to conduct an effective statement analysis, we must approach the statement as fact. The statement (written or verbal) is what the person wants us to know.

This is not to be confused with what I often hear, which is everyone should be believed until we have information or evidence to the contrary. Taking the statement as fact is not the same as believing what is being provided. I accept it as fact because it is to them; it is what they have related regarding the incident. As stated above, I neither believe nor disbelieve. I apply the techniques and see how the statement fairs.

Once an opinion is formed, humans are unlikely to change their minds. We get what is known as "confirmation bias" and ignore evidence that opposes our already formed opinion. The more information you can analyze before determining whether any statement is truthful or deceptive, the more accurate your assessment is likely to be.

Last, as a law enforcement officer for almost thirty-five years, I know how officers as well as many of the people who conduct various investigations like to "connect the dots." In conducting statement analysis, one cannot just connect the dots. The statement must stand on its own. We cannot infer what is being stated, nor can we discount anything that is provided. As an example, I use the frog test:

There are three frogs sitting on a log. One of the frogs decides to jump off. How many frogs are now left on the log?

My students usually hesitate because they anticipate there's some trick. There is no trick.

How many frogs are on the log?

The answer is three. Just because a frog *decided* to jump off the log doesn't mean it did. Otherwise, the statement would read, "One frog jumped off the log"—and it doesn't. This is one of the ways people are deceptive and is an example of connecting dots that aren't actually connected. If you *assumed* the reality of the situation involved two frogs left on the log, have I lied to you? No, not technically. People tend to justify this type of statement because they are not providing false information. It is what I call being *truthfully deceptive.*

All statements represent an edited version of what a subject believes is important. Therefore, if the information is offered, that means it's important to the subject—and should be to us as well. You see, although we may give the direction for people to include as much detail as possible, realize that people are not going to offer a lot of detail. This is particularly true in written statements and another reason why I advocate for obtaining them whenever possible. You see, the information that is provided is telling, whether it is a lot or a little. It's not the length of the statement that is of value; it is the information present as well as the information that isn't present.

In my class, I have students (mostly all law enforcement) write a statement about their most recent day off. I give them the same directions as above. I do this so they have a sample of their own handwriting to use in the graphology section as well as a statement they can refer to as we go through the statement analysis training. I know they are not going to write all of the details about their day off—and they don't. Statements range from a half page to a page and a half. I've not seen one shorter or longer. Why? Because they have edited out anything that was unimportant to them and included only what they determined was important. This practice statement also demonstrates to them that people providing statements on crimes do the exact same thing.

One last thing, much like the section on body language, not everybody does everything. In other words, just because someone didn't go to their liar's triangle doesn't mean they are being truthful. Attention should be given to what they did do. The same thing applies in statement analysis. Not every statement will contain every "red flag" we discuss. The more we know about how people are deceptive, the less the chance someone will get away with their deception.

Okay, with some of the ground rules set, let's get to how we analyze a statement.

Lesson 1: Conducting a Statement Analysis

Length of Statements

If you are looking at a written statement from someone concerning an event, one of the first things you should take note of is the length of the statement. Is it congruent with someone's involvement in the incident? If not, we should ask why.

For example, I was involved in the Casey Anthony investigation. The case received national attention as Casey, along with her parents, George and Cindy, had reported her two-year-old daughter Caylee missing. Months later, her remains were found near the Anthonys' home. Without going into great detail, I was in Internal Affairs at the time, and when the remains of Caylee Anthony were discovered by Roy Kronk, he gave some media interviews. During those interviews, Kronk made disparaging comments regarding our department's response to previous 911 calls for service he'd made. Well, it doesn't take long for comments like that to reach the top, and I was assigned to investigate those prior calls for service.

One of my first orders of business was to meet with the criminal investigators and obtain the statements made by Kronk. At that time, they had obtained one written statement and two audiotaped statements. When I saw the written statement, I thought it was quite short: Kronk had only written four lines. Now, I hadn't expected it to be lengthy, but *still*—four lines was pretty short for someone who'd found human remains. This was my first "red flag" that Kronk might not have been completely forthcoming. This is a good time to tell readers that as I refer to statements, these are actual statements in criminal investigations. Some of the material contained in them may be graphic. A copy of Kronk's statement is below.

I WENT INTO THE WOODS TO URINATE SAW BLACK PLASTIC BAG
HIT WITH STICK SOUNDED LIKE HARD PLASTIC IT WAS ROUND
PULLED BAG WITH STICK BAG OPENED & A SMALL HUMAN SKULL
WITH DUCT TAPE & HAIR STILL ON HEAD DROPPED OUT.

When reviewing written statements from people who had significant involvement in an incident, the statement should usually be about three-quarters of a page to a page and a half. Generally, this will only apply to a victim's statement of the incident—and I've seen thousands of them. If the statement is significantly shorter, it's an indication they are withholding information. If the statement is significantly longer, it's an indication they are trying to convince us of something. Obviously, the statement by Kronk was indicative of someone who was withholding information.

After reviewing the statement along with some other information I had available to me, there was no doubt in my mind that Kronk wasn't being completely honest with the criminal investigators. I spoke with them and detailed my findings. I was certain Kronk had discovered the remains of Caylee in August—four months before the statement was written in December. The criminal investigators agreed to bring Kronk in for another interview, which occurred in January. Soon, Kronk admitted discovering the remains in August. However, go back and take a look at the statement—there is no lie in it. It is *truthfully deceptive*.

Now, there is another measure we can apply for victim statements: the 25-50-25 measure. That means that in truthful statements, most people will spend about 25 percent of the statement before the main issue (or crime) begins. About 50 percent of the statement will cover the main issue, the actual crime. Then the final 25 percent of the statement will document events after the main issue has concluded.

You will find that most deceptive statements don't come close to the 25-50-25. They will mostly have long beginnings before they get to the main issue and abrupt endings. When conducting a statement analysis, if it is a victim statement I'm reviewing, 25-50-25 is my first test.

Let's take a look at a theoretical statement law enforcement might get from a person alleging they were the victim of a robbery:

After I left the club, I drove around a little while and park the car. The car was parked by the 7-Eleven. I had to go to the bathroom, so I walked to an alley up the street from the 7-Eleven. I walked into the alley to go to the bathroom. While I was going to the bathroom, somebody walked up behind me and put what felt like a gun against my back. This person started going through my pockets. I guess while he was going through my pockets, he felt my personal weapon and took it along with $120.

If this victim statement were handwritten, it would be approximately three-quarters of a page to a full page, so it's not particularly short. Note the main issue begins where the statement says, "…somebody walked up behind me" and concludes at the very end of the statement. Without getting into any difficult math, one can easily determine the statement comes nowhere close to the 25-50-25 rule. It's about 50-50-0.

Most deceptive statements tend to begin the main issue more than a third of the way through. The victim is essentially stalling before getting to their main deception; they're just stalling in written format. Most deceptive statements also have abrupt endings. Once the person has gotten through the deception, they end their statement (almost in relief).

There are several other issues with this particular statement—red flags of deception that leave no doubt the statement is deceptive. In cases like this—and many others—I'm not assuming that *nothing* occurred and that the statement is a complete fabrication. As I've stated, that is usually not the case. However, what the red flags point to is deception in the storytelling itself. Remember, it's important to know where to "put your shovel down and dig."

In the lessons ahead, we'll cover more signs we want to pay attention to in statements, some of which are contained in the above statement. If you want to test yourself, go ahead and see if you can identify other areas in the statement that indicate deception. Remember that these aren't lies; instead, they're areas to focus our questions on, for this person *and* any subsequent investigations. I'll refer back to this statement when we cover the other areas we would want to address further. These are areas that indicate this statement is truthfully deceptive.

The First Sentence

If a statement is collected properly and the person was not "coached" on how to write their statement and/or where to start, the first sentence is very significant. Why? Because the person has gone into their memory and determined what the farthest point is from the incident that *still belongs to the incident*. They are telling you where the incident began in their minds. This should not be disregarded. People do this subconsciously when going into their memory to retell a story. Going back to the statement of the robbery, the incident began at the club—and that's where the investigation should begin as well. It's highly likely that was where the victim met the suspect.

The statement below is an actual statement collected in a homicide investigation. The statement is from the victim's husband. Essentially, he claimed they'd been the victims of a home invasion where his wife was shot and killed. Read the statement and try to figure out why he would begin his statement so early. Note that "xx" in the transcription indicates cross-outs.

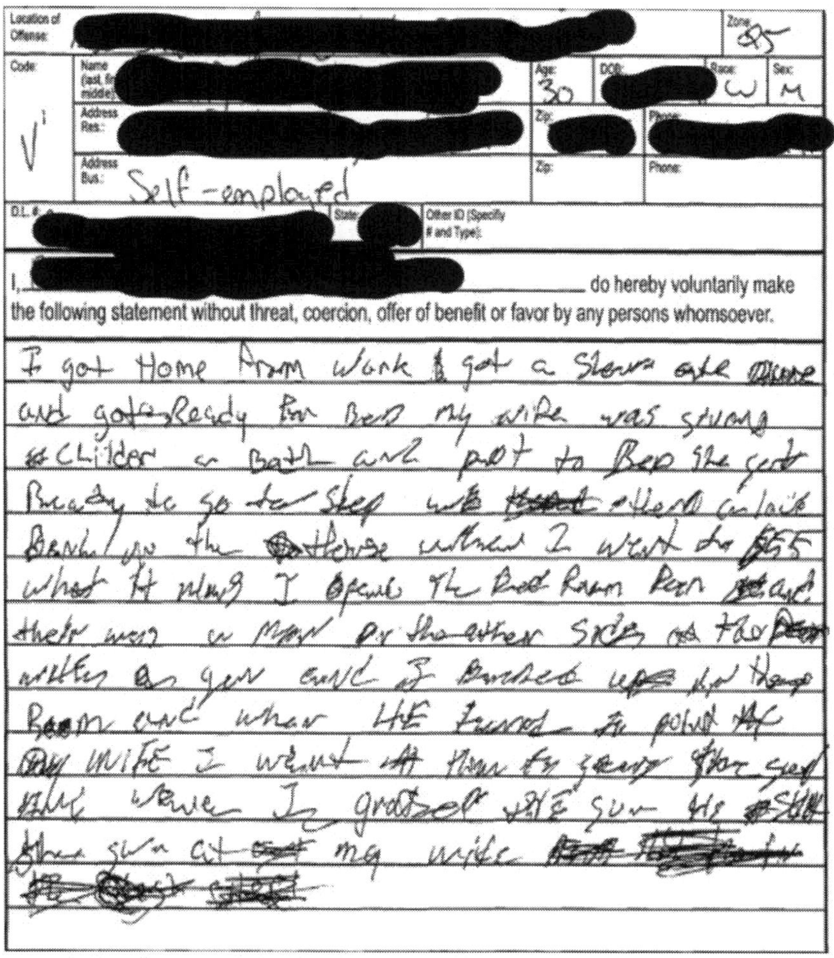

Location of Offense: [redacted] Zone: 85

Code: V

Name (last, first, middle): [redacted] Age: 30 DOB: [redacted] Race: W Sex: M

Address Res.: [redacted] Zip: [redacted] Phone: [redacted]

Address Bus.: Self-employed Zip: Phone:

D.L. #: [redacted] State: [redacted] Other ID (Specify # and Type):

I, [redacted] do hereby voluntarily make the following statement without threat, coercion, offer of benefit or favor by any persons whomsoever.

Transcript

I got home from work xx and got a shower ate xx
and got ready for bed my wife was giving
xx children a bath and put to bed she gets
ready to go to sleep we xx herd a xx

xx on the house I went to see
what it was I opened the bed room door and
there was a man on the other side of the door
with a gun and I backed up in the
room and when he turned to point at
my wife I went thru xx xx
xx xx I grabbed the gun he shot
the gun at my wife xx xx
xx xx xx

The shooting didn't occur until late in the evening, but he began his statement several hours before the shooting, when he'd gotten home from work. If someone were relaying this story truthfully, it's highly unlikely they would begin their statement so early. However, this man shot and killed his wife and was attempting to fabricate a home invasion. He began the story when he got home from work because he went into his memory and asked himself, "Where did this start?" Subconsciously, he knew it began when he arrived home—because that was when he started arguing with his wife.

Note that at the end of his statement he wrote, "I grabbed the gun he shot the gun at my wife." This information is untrue. Without getting into graphology, you can plainly see the difficulty he has in writing something he knows to be deceptive. You don't have to know anything about handwriting to see the stress—the writing is significantly different from the writing at the beginning.

As this is also a statement of someone who had significant involvement in an incident and was claiming to be a victim, we can also apply the 25-50-25 formula. Note it is a twelve-line statement, and the main issue begins at line seven. It's basically 50-50-0. It fails that test, and the chances are high that it's a deceptive statement.

The Social Introduction

We should never ignore how someone is introduced. Whether it is in writing or a verbal statement, the subject is telling us about their relationships. When conducting investigations, this information is key. If the person doesn't tell us someone is their husband, wife, son, or daughter in their language, it speaks to a troubled relationship.

Basically, there are three parts to a social introduction. They are:

- Possession
- Title
- Name

Three checkmarks indicate a very good relationship. Two checkmarks are good. One checkmark signals trouble, and no checkmarks tells me it's not a healthy relationship. That means it's an area I want to explore—a good place to put my shovel down and dig.

Let me explain further. If I were in a classroom and my wife were suddenly to appear at the door, I would introduce her to the class. I might say something like, "Everyone, this is my wife, Julie." This is an indication of a good relationship—Julie got three checkmarks:

- Possession: "my"
- Title: "wife"
- Name: "Julie"

Now, I could introduce her by saying, "This is my wife." That's not too bad. Julie got two checkmarks. She got possession and title but no name. Similarly, I could say, "This is Julie." There, Julie only got one checkmark. She got a name but no possession or title. I could also state, "This is the wife." Again, one checkmark. This is not a sign of a good relationship. Of course, once the person is introduced, the language can be shortened since there is no longer a need to re-introduce the person. Please note that the social introduction can be analyzed when it is in both verbal and written forms.

A few years ago, we responded to a shooting. It was reported as a possible suicide where a pregnant woman had shot herself in the presence of her husband. Below is the actual statement he offered. After the actual statement, you will see a transcript:

Orange County Sheriff's Office

STATEMENT
Please fill out in full detail

Date of Affidavit: Month 11 Day 14 Year 2013 Time 1835

Offense: DEATH INV

Date of Offense: Month 11 Day 14 Year 2013 Time 1627

Code: WIT

I, ________ do hereby voluntarily make the following statement without threat, coercion, offer of benefit or favor by any persons whomsoever.

~List stolen items separately (with values) in body of statement.~

Total Value of Property Stolen/Damaged $

I have reviewed the Victim's Rights package.

I will testify in court

I will prosecute criminally

Sworn To and Subscribed Before Me This 14 day of November, 20 13

I Swear/Affirm the Above and/or Attached Statements are Correct and True.

Signature:

Personally Known / Produced Identification

Deputy Sheriff / Notary Public

Type of ID: NJ DL

Page 1 of 1

Transcript

I was sitting in the living room she asked me to see my work gun
I said yes I gave it to her I sat back over at chair and heard gun
go off I keep ammo in gun but no round in chamber. I turned
around and saw her I got up out chair and saw her I said Lexi
she didn't respond I saw her I took the gun out of her right hand. I saw
blood out her nose I I moved out to hallway screaming dad and he was there
he called police Dad said give me the gun and I handed it to him the gun is
issued from my job G45 Alexis is my wife we've been together since November
2011 we've been married for one year I've been living here since July 2013.

Notice that on the very first line, he introduces the reader to his wife. He refers to her as "she." This tells me that they did not have a good relationship, crucial information when investigating a case of this nature. I explored their relationship further and put my shovel down right there.

The man soon confessed to shooting and killing his wife. The relationship had been in trouble, and they had both suspected the other of adultery. People tell us about relationships through their social introductions—if we are paying attention.

Of course, like the other statements we've already seen, this is not the only red flag present. Take another look. This isn't a victim statement or someone who claims to have had significant involvement, so I can't apply the 25-50-25 rule. In the first six lines of the statement, there are thirteen instance of the personal pronoun "I." An overuse of this personal pronoun is an indication of anxiety. There are also repeated phrases present in the statement. Repeated phrases are also a sign of stress and likely in place of other information the person doesn't want you to know. We'll discuss these principles in more depth in later lessons.

Several red flags all point in the same direction: the statement is very likely deceptive. If I follow the clues provided by an analysis, when I arrive at a scene and read a statement like this, I know where to direct my inquiries. My investigation has focus, and I know what questions I want to ask. I have "inside knowledge" due to my experience and training with statement analysis, knowledge I use to assist me in conducting a complete and thorough investigation.

Personal Dictionaries

Personal dictionaries are important because they facilitate truthful deception. A personal dictionary is just that—it's someone's own personal definition of a word that may differ from ours. Due to their personal dictionaries, a person can give a response to a question that may sound truthful, but in fact is deceptive. Here are some examples:

- "I didn't steal the money."
- "I didn't punch anyone."
- "I did not have sexual relations with that woman."

You see, each of these denials contains a key word that may use someone's unique definition of that term. For instance, if someone intended to pay the money back, well, they weren't actually "stealing" it, were they?

You may remember Lance Armstrong. Do you think Lance would consider himself a cheater? Of course not! Armstrong rationalized his conduct through his personal dictionary. In fact, Armstrong previously explained that he looked up the word "cheat," and it meant "to gain an unfair advantage." Well, if *many* people are engaging in the conduct, it's not an unfair advantage, is it? Armstrong was just leveling the playing field. Armstrong would definitely not consider himself a cheater—due to his personal dictionary. If you were to ask Armstrong to take a polygraph and that question were asked, I doubt he would fail that question. I also suspect that many athletes who use performance-enhancing drugs rationalize their conduct in much the same manner.

Recognize that last example from the above list? Yeah, probably. That was the initial response by former President Bill Clinton in his denial of an affair with Monica Lewinsky. His answer depends on your definition of "sexual relations." If, in your personal dictionary, you don't consider their behavior to be sexual relations, you could provide this explanation. Is it a lie? No, it isn't—all because of Clinton's personal dictionary. It is truthfully deceptive. In fact, in his admission, Clinton later admitted that his initial defense hadn't been "completely truthful."

Many words can fall into a personal dictionary. This is why we need to pay attention to the words people choose, and if someone were to use a word they could define differently, then that would be a good place to put our shovel down to dig a little deeper.

Most people have an aversion to lying. By continuing to explore this area and ask questions, we force people to either lie or come clean and be truthful. Knowing the next question to ask is a significant part of being a good detector of deceit, such as in the previous example of the husband who shot his wife. When we interviewed him, we wanted to ask about his relationship with his wife and exactly what had been going on. The red flag was there. In the case of a personal dictionary, it's another flag. Obtain additional information and have the person clarify exactly what they meant by the word they used.

Repeating Words/Phrases

When someone repeats a word or a phrase in a written or verbal statement, it's a sign of anxiety. When we put the anxiety in the context of a criminal investigation or even a conversation, it could indicate deception. This sign in particular, as well as some of the others, typically flies under the radar. We've already seen some repeated phrases in previous statements. Not many people catch these in speech or writing.

Below is an actual statement in a shooting investigation. The writer went to the hospital and dropped off his friend, who had been shot. When the officer at the hospital asked him what had happened, this is the statement he wrote. The friend later died from his injuries. See if you can spot the deception. Do you know where to put your shovel? The transcribed version will follow the written statement.

Orange County Sheriff's Office

STATEMENT

Please fill out in full detail.

Date of Affidavit: 06/07/13 0350

Offense: Agg Battery w/ Firearm

Location of Offense: Rose Bv./S. Rio Grande Av.

Age: 26

Zone: 43

W M

1301 Rose Bv.

32831

I, ______ do hereby voluntarily make the following statement without threat, coercion, offer of benefit or favor by any persons whomsoever.

Me and my friends where hanging out at my house when I whent inside to check on the score Spurs where beating Miami I stay inside for about 20 min when I came out side Jason was not there but his car was I guess he was drunk So I desided to go to Chevron on RioGrande and Oak Ridge to get cigarettes when I stopped on Richmond ... and Rose I seen a body laying down on RioGrande and Rose ... I pulled to the side and discovered it was my friend Jason I pulled to the side and grabed him ... him in the car and whent straight to Emergency on the way here I aske him ... and he could not answere me So I brought him straight to the Emergency room.

List stolen items separately (with values) in body of statement.

Total Value of Property Stolen/Damaged: $ 0

I have reviewed the Victim's Rights package.

I will testify in court.

I will prosecute criminally.

Sworn To and Subscribed Before Me This 7 day of ______ 20 13

Personally Known ☐

Produced Identification ☑

Type of ID: FL ID

Deputy Sheriff ☐ Notary Public ☐

I Swear/Affirm the Above and/or Attached Statements are Correct and True.

Signature:

Page 1 of 1

Transcript

Me and my friends were hanging out at my house when I went inside to check on the score Spurs where beating Miami I stay inside for about 20 min when I came out side Jason was not there but his car was I guess he was drunk so I decided to go to Chevron on Rio Grande and Oak Ridge to get cigarettes

> when I stoped on Rio Grande and Rose I seen a body
> laying down on Rio Grande and Rose blvd I pulled
> to the side and discovered it was my friend Jason
> I pulled to the side and grabbed him pulled him
> in the car and whent straight to the emergency
> on the way here I asked him what happened
> and he could not answer me so I brought him
> straight to the emergency room.

Note that there are a few repeated phrases in this statement: "on Rio Grande and Rose" is written twice. Farther down in the statement, "straight to the emergency" is also written twice. These are an indicators of anxiety—and, yes, anxiety because the writer wasn't being completely forthcoming. In his statement, he led the reader to believe the shooting may have occurred near Rio Grande and Rose Boulevard. Did it?

Years later, an informant came forward and reported he'd been present the night the victim had been shot. The informant related that the subject and the victim had been playing with a firearm when it had gone off, accidentally shooting the victim. The writer had felt bad, so he had taken him to the hospital to get him medical attention.

During the initial investigation, officers attempted to locate a scene near Rio Grande and Rose. They didn't find any evidence of a shooting. Look again where the writer began his statement: at his house. This is also where the informant later admitted the shooting took place. The writer went into his memory and decided that was the moment farthest from the incident that still belonged to the incident.

If the officers or investigators who had responded to this particular crime had been aware of these indicators—the deception flags found in the repeated phrases and the first sentence—they might have gone to the writer's residence. If they had, they probably would have located evidence of the shooting and been on their way to solving the case. They didn't. Remember that 5.2 percent higher clearance rate? This statement was sitting in the case file all along.

Delaying Phrases

When a difficult question is asked, a subject may respond with something like the following:

- Where did you hear that?
- Could you be more specific?
- Can you repeat the question?
- Do I know anything about…?

Phrases such as this buy the person time to think about how they want to answer the question, which must have been a sensitive one. Remember—as mentioned in the section on body language—the longer it takes for the person to respond to a question, the less reliable the information. Delaying phrases gives an increase in time, and the information that follows should be carefully considered.

"Extra" Words

Don't overlook "extra" words people may include that don't change a statement's meaning. Some examples are:

- "I actually haven't seen Jim in a week."
- "I really don't know anything."

There's a reason people include these "extra" words: it's another sign of anxiety and a break from the "norm," or normal way in which people would usually state something. Much like we covered with body language, deception stress leaks out into human behavior.

One of the examples I use in class is of a man testifying in court about the murder of his wife. The brief clip is taken from the outstanding documentary *Murder on a Sunday Morning.* The couple had been walking back to their room when they'd been approached by a man with a firearm attempting a robbery. While on the stand, the man provided an account of the event, and when he described the actions of his wife, he stated: "She first said 'oh' and started taking off her purse to give it to him."

What was he saying here? Can you detect the deception?

There are two "extra" words he included in his recounting of the event, "first" and "started." Why did he include those words? He could have said the same thing by stating, "She took off her purse and gave it to him" or "She took off her purse to give it to him."

But he didn't. He added extra words. Remember the information I offered earlier—a statement is an edited version of what the person believes to be important. If it wasn't important, then he wouldn't have said it (or written it).

So why are these extra words important? Let's take a closer look. There isn't a "first" without a second. If someone says they first did something, there is always another action that followed. Do we know where to put our shovel? The follow-up question he should have been asked was "What else did your wife say?"

In answering that question, he is faced with a dilemma. He either needs to lie to us, or he is going to tell the truth. Later in the documentary, it's revealed that his wife also called the man a racial slur.

Let's take a look at the next extra word—"started." If I tell you I *started* to mow my lawn on Saturday, I'm communicating to you that something interrupted me. I didn't complete the job without interruption, or I would have said, "I mowed my lawn on Saturday." Do we know where to put our shovel? The follow-up should have been "What else happened when she was taking her purse off?" It's later revealed that his wife threw her hot cup of coffee in the suspect's face.

Now, is this incident still an armed robbery that escalated into a homicide? Yes, it is. However, we can now build a case formed on a solid foundation and not half-truths.

Just as importantly, when I interview a suspect using these skills, I figure out things that only he would know. I can also use this information to offer him some justification for his actions during the interrogation. If I don't know this information, it could hinder my ability to obtain an admission or confession.

Remember: nothing the man stated was a lie. It was truthfully deceptive.

Articles

This is another aspect of statement analysis that often goes unnoticed. Is there a difference between these two sentences?

- A man raped me.
- The man raped me.

If you hear the first, that's a strong indicator that the attacker was unknown to the victim. If you hear the second sentence, the use of the article "the" is a strong indicator that it was somebody the victim knew.

When I went back to Homicide as the sergeant, there was an unsolved murder case of a young man. His father called me numerous times to berate me about the investigation and wanted to know what progress was being made. By this time, the case was over a year old and was no longer being actively investigated because there were no new leads. I asked the detective to brief me so I could speak to the victim's father.

It turned out that the victim had asked a young lady out for a lunch date. They had ridden on his motorcycle, and he had dropped her off at her house. As they'd been talking by the motorcycle, a van had turned on to the street and driven past them. It had pulled to the side, and a man had gotten out with a firearm. The victim had run but had still been shot and killed in the front yard.

Well, the victim's father continued to call. I finally asked the detective for his case file so I could take a closer look. One of the first things I did was listen to the audiotaped interview that the detective had conducted with the young lady at the scene—it's common for detectives to audiotape interviews at scenes even if there is an accompanying written statement.

I listened to the woman describe the event in the twenty-minute taped interview. I heard her state, "…the motorcycle, just talking for a little bit before I went inside. So I see, uh, the van coming down from this way, coming down that way. I didn't, we didn't think, you know, anything, so we just continued…"

The first time she mentioned the van, she stated "*the* van" not "*a* van." If the woman had never seen the van before, it would have been *a* van. This is a strong and significant indicator the woman had indeed seen the van previously. And if she'd known the van, she'd probably known who had been in the van.

I called the case detective to my office and directed him to re-interview her, as I believed she'd recognized the vehicle. He informed me that she'd moved out of state; I directed him to locate her and conduct another interview. He did. The woman admitted she had known the van, and it had been her former boyfriend who'd exited the van and shot the victim. She explained she was afraid of him and had been too scared to tell the truth at the time.

Had she lied? No, she hadn't. She'd been truthfully deceptive, but her words still gave her away. If that detective had known and utilized the skills of statement analysis, he may have been aware of the same clues. Do we know where to put our shovel? Yes, the next question to her should have been, "Tell me more about this van; have you seen it somewhere before?" Again, she would've had to lie or tell the truth.

Despite her revised statement, the state attorney's office refused to prosecute the case because they deemed she lacked credibility in the eyes of the court. Something as simple as "a" and "the" could have made the difference between a closed case and an unsolved case. Remember that 5.2 percent?

Possession

Pay attention to what the person takes possession of in their statement. In his book *I Want to Tell You*, O.J. Simpson states, "I am grateful that even those who believe in my guilt also believe that I should have my day in court and have agreed to let their words be published in this book."

Note that Simpson takes ownership of *his* "guilt."

When referring to a car, does the average person call it *my* car or *the* car? If I see "the car" on a statement, one of the first questions I'm going to ask is whether we have checked the car's registration (most of the time, it's one of the first thing officers will do). If the car is registered to the person who wrote "the car" in their statement, that's a red flag. Why isn't it "*my* car"? Almost certainly, the person wants to distance themselves from something about it. Now, if the car *doesn't* belong to the person (perhaps it's a company car, or the car is registered to a family member), then there is some explanation as to why it wasn't "my car."

Possession is a good place to put your shovel down and dig.

Emotions

Where speakers insert emotional components into a story is also significant. A truthful person tends to describe the emotions connected to an event after it has occurred. A deceptive person tends to mention emotions after the incident has occurred or not at all.

The deceptive person might have never truly experienced the emotions connected with the incident, so they may "forget" to mention them. If they do remember to mention emotions, it is usually *during* the time of the incident because that's where they think people expect to hear them. However, it's not where the emotions were truly experienced in the truthful telling of a story.

In my career, I've been involved in many investigations regarding the use of deadly force. Officers involved in deadly force encounters are often defending themselves from an attack. These officers and their interviewers play a game during the interview. At some point during the interview, the officer will almost invariably state something to the effect of "I was in fear for my life" at the time they used the deadly force (usually their firearms).

I've known many officers personally—and many who have attended my training classes—who have found themselves in circumstances requiring the use of deadly force. No matter the state they come from, they all know that the magic words are "I was in fear for my life." My follow-up question to them is "Was that truly the emotion you were experiencing at the moment you used deadly force?" Now, the question is rhetorical; I don't expect an answer. But I see the eyebrows go up and the expressions on their faces. At that moment, they were fighting back; they were responding to the threat. There was no time to experience the emotion of fear.

The fact is that officers who use deadly force are responding to a threat they are facing at that moment. They are fighting back as they have been trained to do when confronted with an attack that could result in their death or the death of someone else. They don't have time to be afraid. But stating those things doesn't play well on Main Street. The state attorney's office, their agency, and the public want to hear that they were "in fear," and that was why they used deadly force. Were they fearful *after* the incident about what could have happened? Yes, in all likelihood. In retrospect, they may think about almost having lost their lives, how difficult the situation had been, and then experience the emotion of fear. But fear is simply not the emotion that is experienced in that moment.

Think about the many horror movies that are shown on television and the movies. When the victim (usually the hero or heroine) of the movie is engaged in the moment of fighting back against the attacker, would you say fear is the emotion they are experiencing at that very moment? Or would it more likely be the emotion of anger? Survival? Or passion?

Another example of emotional storytelling in deception comes from New York Representative Alexandria Ocasio-Cortez as she relayed her "harrowing" experience of what happened to her on January 6, 2021, during the riot at the Capitol. Shortly after the incident, Ocasio-Cortez released a video recapping her day. Much of the media immediately picked up the dramatic clip and emphasized that Ocasio-Cortez was lucky to have escaped harm. During the video, Ocasio-Cortez describes a banging on her office door and states, "This was the moment where I thought everything was over. I just happen to be a spiritual person and raised in that context, and I really just felt like, you know, if this is the plan for me…then people will be able to take it from here."

Many in the media and celebrities lauded her for her bravery and apparent selflessness as she endured this experience. I recall when I first saw the video, I immediately knew it was deceptive. First, there are unnecessary "extra" words: "really" and "you know." Next, and more importantly, if someone is truthfully relaying an incident such as this, they generally aren't thinking,

"...if this is the plan for me, people will be able to take it from here." A truthful person would be attempting to get to a place of safety or potentially think of how they could defend themselves—thanks to the "fight-or-flight" response. It's deceptive, but that's where deceptive people think the emotions should be. It isn't where truthful people really experience them.

You may recall that it was later revealed Ocasio-Cortez's office building is located quite a distance away from the Capitol. In addition, the Capitol was not breached until hours after Ocasio-Cortez's building had already been evacuated. So how could Ocasio-Cortez have been so afraid of an event which hadn't yet occurred? She wasn't; it was a deceptive retelling of the event for political purposes.

Missing Time and Loss of Memory

When someone includes words that indicate missing time in their story, it's a good idea to go back and fill in the time gap. Some of these words include:

- After, afterward
- Sometime later
- The next thing I knew
- Later on

The issue with these words is that they affect a timeline and indicate something has been skipped over. If I'm talking to my son, and he states, "Later on, we went to the movie," I'm not going to press him for additional details. However, timelines can be crucial in criminal or administrative investigations, and an investigator should take a subject back through their timeline to fill in the gap.

Another tactic subjects may use to avoid details they'd rather not communicate is to claim memory loss. Watch for "I don't recall" or "I can't remember" cards. If you hear these phrases, it is likely someone who does not want to provide details. Now, there's a difference between this as a response to a question versus in an open statement. For instance, if someone responds "I don't know" to a direct question, they might genuinely not know; if they randomly suggest they don't know certain details before questions are posed, that's a red flag. After all, doesn't someone need to remember what they forgot in order to state they don't recall something? You don't remember what you don't remember.

But if someone states either verbally or in writing, "I don't recall what clothing the suspect was wearing," this is a sign of deception. Why would someone include in their statement what they don't recall? Truthful people don't include what they don't remember.

The fact is that we only recall a handful or so of instances in our lives where a traumatic event left a significant impression on us. For instance, I can't tell you what I had for lunch last Monday, but I *can* tell you who I was with and where I was on 9/11. I can also give you the same details when the Challenger exploded. I can recall details of a car accident I was involved in at seventeen.

Similarly, I would be able to remember someone who pointed a gun at me or committed a sexual battery against me. Why? Because when someone is personally involved in a traumatic experience, it's one of those events that becomes etched in our memories. We have the ability to recall what we saw, what we heard, and even what we smelled in those rare moments. It's also why hearing a certain song takes you back to a certain memory, and smelling a certain scent may bring back an image.

There is a specific type of interview called the cognitive interview. It's designed to incorporate all five senses in order to enable a person to better recall details they otherwise might not remember. There may be some who have legitimately blocked out events from their memory, but those are the exception, not the rule. Deceptive people often use the lost memory card simply because they don't want to furnish additional details regarding an event.

Cross Outs

Cross outs are also something that shouldn't be disregarded in statements. Obviously, this would only apply to written statements, but it's another good reason to collect written statements as a routine practice in investigations. How a word or words are crossed out may indicate anxiety on the part of the writer. That anxiety could be because the person is being deceptive.

For instance, if a word or words have one or two horizontal slashes due to a spelling error, it can be disregarded. It's also not a concern because the writer knows the reader will be able to read what they wrote. But if it's a scrawled scratch-out of a word or words, the question is worth asking—why was it important to the writer that I not be able to read what they wrote? Scratching things out in that manner is a sign of anxiety. When it comes to providing information as it relates to an investigation, that could very well be a sign of deception.

Can you make out what was written? Those words may be the truth leaking into an otherwise deceptive statement. When I was working violent crimes investigations, I responded to a report from the local college of an armed robbery. Students alleged their laptops had been stolen. When I arrived, I reviewed the written statements taken by the responding officers.

When I reviewed these particular statements, I noticed several words had been scratched out. As you sometimes can, I could read what had been written underneath. While I don't specifically recall what was written, it wasn't something consistent with the allegation of an armed robbery. I called the young man over to me and asked him why he wrote what he did. He denied writing it. I retorted that he indeed wrote it but scratched it out. Again, he stammered and denied having written it.

This was an example of the truth leaking into a deceptive statement. He had attempted to scratch it out so the information couldn't be read. I cautioned the man that if he were going to be dishonest, it was a crime to file a false police report or to provide false information. He soon decided he no longer wanted to cooperate with the investigation.

Contractions

Perhaps the most common and among the most significant signs of deception is a lack of contractions. This sign is most commonly associated with verbal deception, although it can also be present in written statements. There are a few reasons for this. Remember when we talked about "norming" where it concerns body language? Behavior that breaks from the norm is significant and should be paid attention to. Well, using that same logic, it's normal in our culture to use contractions. For instance:

"I don't know where John lives," as opposed to "I do not know where John lives."

"I didn't steal any of the missing money," as opposed to "I did not steal any of the missing money."

"I wouldn't cheat on my taxes," as opposed to "I would not cheat on my taxes."

Note the first statement in each example is normal for the vast majority of people in the US. So if someone were to *not* use the contraction, as in the second statement in each example, it would represent a break from the norm and would be associated with deception.

Another reason why deceitful people tend to drop contractions in their speech is that they want to seem more emphatic in their denials, but this has the opposite effect. Keep in mind that you must determine whether a person's failure to use contractions is part of their normal speech pattern. For instance, when learning to speak English, non-native speakers may have been taught to not use contractions. It would then be a norm for that person and should not be counted as a sign of deception. In addition, when someone is trying to stress a point or be emphatic, they may not use contractions. It is in the instance of a denial that it is unnecessary. The deceptive tend to do this as they want to be emphatic in their denial when it isn't necessary.

Examples of this principle are everywhere. Listen for a person's lack of contractions in their denials, and you'll hear it more than you think. Of course, we can go back to a previous quote regarding personal dictionaries to find an example of a lack of contractions. You will recall when Former President Clinton stated, "I did not have sexual relations with that woman, Miss Lewinski."

The former president's statement included *two* red flags: a personal dictionary and a dropped contraction. As I mentioned earlier, the more red flags we spot, the more certain we can be of deception. You'll find this clue to deception very helpful as you listen when someone drops their use of contractions. While it's particularly helpful in a denial, if a person is providing you with purportedly truthful information and you hear contractions missing, pay close attention to the information being given.

Statements in the Negative

Statements in the negative are just that. They are statements of what *didn't* occur. Strange, huh? People do this on a regular basis, so let's talk about why they are important. First, a couple of things to remember when dealing with these statements: this can only be noted as a sign of deception if it is *not* in response to a question, and it must be in what is known as an open, or volunteered, statement—for example, in a written statement in a criminal investigation, someone might make a point of writing about something that *didn't* occur.

In my class, students write statements about their most recent day off. Now, these students have nothing of immediate importance or significance to write about, but *not one* has ever written what they didn't do on their day off. Why? Because a statement is a statement of what *did* occur, not what didn't occur. One of the points I stress to them is when they read or hear someone say what they *didn't* do, I want them to recall their own statements. They had nothing to write about and didn't include this type of information, so why would this person do the opposite when they did have something important to write about? Hint: they've included it because it *did* occur.

Let me offer a few examples. In December 2008, I became involved in the Casey Anthony investigation. Many will recall when Casey Anthony and her parents reported her daughter, Caylee, missing. Caylee's remains were found a few months later by a meter reader named Roy Kronk. Well, I was in our Internal Affairs section at the time. When he found human remains, the media descended on the area and Roy Kronk like an army. It wasn't long before they were able to get Roy to give a statement.

During that statement, Kronk couldn't resist making some disparaging comments about the sheriff's office. As many of you know, it doesn't take long for comments like that to get to the top. Kronk alleged that officers had failed to properly do their jobs on previous calls he had placed. It became my job to investigate those prior calls for service to find out precisely what Kronk was referring to.

It turned out that Kronk had called 911 in August (four months before discovering the remains in December). One of the first things I did was review his 911 calls. In those calls, Kronk related something he had seen in a wooded area that "didn't seem to belong." He made several interesting statements. Among them, he stated, "I don't know what it is." Roy also stated, "I didn't touch anything" and "I'm not going in that…"

I noted that these statements were in the negative. They were unsolicited statements—not in response to any question he had been asked. Now, if there had only been one statement, I probably would have overlooked it. But multiple negative statements along with the other facts of the case soon led me to believe Kronk wasn't being completely truthful with the criminal investigators.

Now, Kronk's honesty wasn't the focus of my investigation, but it also wasn't something I could overlook. After sharing my initial observations with my supervisor, I went and discussed my concerns with the detectives conducting the criminal investigation.

As a result, Kronk was called back in to speak with the detectives in January 2009. It wasn't long before Kronk admitted that he had indeed found the remains in August, as I suspected. This is probably a good time to interject that neither I nor the detective told Kronk, "Look, you made a few statements in the negative that caused us to believe you weren't being truthful." Instead, we used the analysis of Kronk's own statements as an indicator he wasn't being completely honest, and good interview skills then confirmed our suspicions.

When someone provides you with negative claims in an open statement, you can almost assuredly turn it around and put it in the positive. It's what they did. Below is a statement taken by a fellow officer from another agency. He was investigating an allegation of a sexual battery, and below is the statement of the suspect. The victim in this case was a friend of the suspect's daughter. A transcribed version will follow the written statement.

without threat, coercion, offer of benefit, or favor by any persons whomsoever

The night that this happen, Its was and house full of People
I was upstair with my wife looking at T.V. Went out to
the store Came back end name deleted was xx looking T.V.
I pass right by her xx on my way upstair. I didnt
thouch her, I was in my room with my wife all night long.
She been an part of my family since the being. Never had
I put my hands on her. xx On the night all I did was take
them to the fair and pick them up. Dont know where all of
this stuff is coming xx from I am trying to get to the bottom
of all this to put this to rest. All this is new to me never
heard this before today.

Sworn to and subscribed before me, this 23 day of April 2011

Transcript

The night that this happen, Its was and house full of people
I was upstair with my wife looking at T.V. Went out to
the store Came back and (name deleted) was xx looking T.V
I pass right by her xx on my way upstair. I didn't
thouch her, I was in my room with my wife all night long.
She been an part of my family since the being. Never had
I put my hands on her. Xx On the night all I did was take
them to the fair and pick them up. Don't know where all of
this stuff is coming xx from. I am trying to get to the bottom
of all this to put this to rest. All this is new to me never
heard this before today.

You can see that he wrote, "I didn't touch her, I was in my room with my wife all night long." He followed that up with the statement, "Never had I put my hands on her." This is clearly information in the negative given in an open statement. Remember, whether it is in a written or verbal statement, information in the negative should be carefully considered. In this particular case, it's a big red flag because the information concerns whether he touched her. There are several other red flags present in the statement; can you spot them?

One we have covered is the cross outs. This is a sign of anxiety in the writer, and in this case, it's because of deception. Another sign is one we haven't covered yet, but we'll get there shortly.

In this particular case, the man admitted to what he had done and wrote a follow-up statement. That statement is below, followed by the transcript.

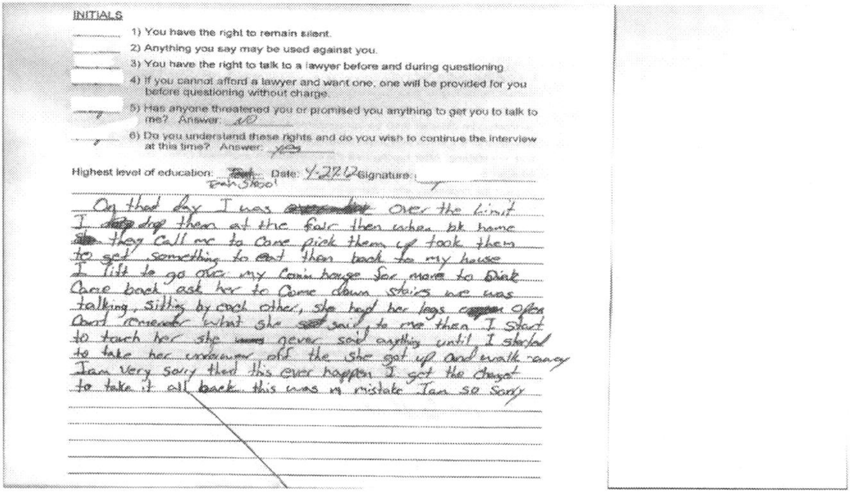

INITIALS

1) You have the right to remain silent.
2) Anything you say may be used against you.
3) You have the right to talk to a lawyer before and during questioning
4) If you cannot afford a lawyer and want one, one will be provided for you before questioning without charge.
5) Has anyone threatened you or promised you anything to get you to talk to me? Answer: NO
6) Do you understand these rights and do you wish to continue the interview at this time? Answer: yes

Highest level of education: xx High School Date: 4-22-12 Signature:

On that day I was xx over the limit
I xx drop them at the fair then when bk home
xx they call me to come pick them up took them
to get something to eat then back to my house
I lift to go over my conin house for more to drink
Came back ask her to come down stairs we was
talking, sitting by each other, she had her legs xx open
can't remember what she xx said to me then I start
to touch her she xx never said anything until I started
to take her xx off the she got up and walk away
I am very sorry that this ever happen I got the chance
to take it all back this was my mistake I am so sorry

Transcript

On that day I was xx over the limit
I xx drop them off at the fair then when bk home
xx they call me to come pick them up took them
to get something to eat then back to my house
I lift to go over my conin house for more to drink
Came back ask her to come down stairs we was
talking, sitting by each other, she had her legs xx open
can't remember what she xx said to me then I start

to touch her she xx never said anything until I started
to take her underwear off the she got up and walk away
I am very sorry that this ever happen I get the chance
to take it all back. This was a mistake I am so sorry

As you can read, he admits to all of the things he previously wrote didn't happen. While it *is* a confession, there are still some issues with this statement, as he's attempting to minimize what occurred. Signs of his anxiety are still present in the cross outs.

Tense

There are three types of tense: past, present, and future. The tense a person uses in relating an event is very significant and should not be overlooked. Tense applies whether you are reviewing a written statement or listening to verbal details of an event. I'll take a look at each tense one at a time to be sure I'm clear on how they affect the veracity of a statement.

Past Tense

A truthful story should generally be in past tense if the event concerns something that happened in the past. Now, if a subject uses past tense in reference to a victim who is still presumed to be alive, this is an indicator the subject has knowledge that the victim is no longer living. I'll provide a few examples of this.

In August 2018, Chris Watts claimed his wife and two daughters were missing. A few days into the investigation, Watts decided to give a media interview. During it, Chris Watts made the following statement: "Yeah…Bella was going to start kindergarten next Monday."

In this case, Watts used past tense, which is normally fine when talking about an event that occurred in the past. However, at this point in his statement, he was talking about something that was supposed to happen in their family's future—his daughter Bella starting kindergarten. Watts stated Bella *was* going to start kindergarten. How did he know she wouldn't start kindergarten the following week? Allegedly, his wife and daughters had only recently gone missing, and there was certainly no bloody scene or any reason to believe they were deceased.

But Chris Watts knew they were deceased. And he knew Bella wasn't going to be starting kindergarten the next week. His hidden knowledge regarding where they really were altered the way he offered this information.

You see, when you fabricate a story like Chris Watts, you have to remember what information you shouldn't know and edit the responses you give. This can be very difficult to do and often results in incorrect tense usage.

Present Tense

When someone uses present tense, it's an indication they are making the story up on the spot. Memory comes from reality, what actually happened. When you have no memory of an event, you need to fabricate it instead. However, as I just mentioned, most people need to do this in real time when deceiving, so they must try to remember that it occurred in the past—although they are making it up right now. Let's take a look at an example.

In her first interview with police concerning her missing daughter, Casey Anthony provided the following statement. Keep in mind—this is only a portion of her statement taken from her audio-recorded interview:

"I got off work—left Universal, driving back to pick up Caylee like a normal day. And I show up to the apartment, knock on the door, and nobody answers. So I call Zeneida's cell phone, and it's out of service. It says the phone is no longer in service, excuse me? So I sit down on the steps and wait for a little bit to see if maybe it was just a fluke, if something happened, and time passed, and I didn't hear from anyone. No one showed up to the house, so I went over to J. Blanchard Park and checked a couple of other places where maybe possibly they would have gone. Couple stores, just regular places that I know Zeneida shops at and she's taken Caylee before."

Do you see the deception? Yes, Casey spoke in present tense! This is an indication it didn't really happen as she said. Some of you might be thinking, though, "Well, this could just be the way she talks." I would respond by pointing out that Casey clearly knows the difference because the statements contain several words in the past tense: "didn't," "showed," "happened," "passed." Nope, Casey was being deceptive.

Future Tense

Future tense can also be an indicator of deception. Usually, this is found in the form of a denial that is meant to sound emphatic. The key word to remember pertaining to this type of deception is the word "would." "Would" is future tense, so someone making a denial using this is not really denying anything that has occurred in the past; they are denying whether they *would* do it in the future. For instance:

"Why would I take any money from the register?"

"I would never steal anything!"

"Why would I do such a thing?"

Future tense-based deceptions occur on a regular basis and, like the other tense deceptions, often go unnoticed because they're disguised as an emphatic denial. Few were more emphatic in their denials than Lance Armstrong and his denials of doping. In one of his many interviews, Armstrong stated, "If you consider my situation, a guy who comes back from, arguably, you know, a death sentence. Why would I then enter into a sport and dope myself up and risk my life again? That's crazy, I would never do that, no, no way."

Personal Pronoun "I"

Seeing or hearing the personal pronoun "I" in someone's statement is important—it's an indication they are taking ownership of their statement, and that's a good thing. In written statements, look for the "I" in the first sentence or two. I've seen statements that didn't contain a personal pronoun "I" throughout its entirety. This is unusual; it's certainly a red flag of deception.

This is yet another sign that can be easily overlooked. I always say the personal pronoun "I" should be sprinkled throughout the statement, sort of like seasoning. There shouldn't be too little or too much. If seasoning is too sparse or too concentrated, the "dish" doesn't taste quite right. If you take a look back at Roy Kronk's written statement under the "Length of Statements" section, you'll find there is only one personal pronoun "I." Roy starts his statement with the personal pronoun, but then there are no more.

So why is that? You'll see as you read the statement that there are "missing" personal pronouns. Subconsciously, when someone wants to subconsciously distance themselves from their statement, they will omit the word "I."

The obvious question then becomes "Why are they distancing themselves from their statement?" Often, it's because the statement is deceptive. Generally speaking, people have an aversion to being deceptive: it makes them uncomfortable and creates anxiety. Although Kronk's written statement doesn't contain a lie or anything technically untrue, it is nonetheless deceptive and caused him to want to distance himself from the statement.

On the reverse side of that, you can have an overuse of the personal pronoun "I." This is another indicator of anxiety, potentially due to deception. The following is taken from the actual court testimony of a police officer who was accused of planting an explosive device. He also happened to be the one to find the explosive, which didn't look too great to the court. Here's what he said:

"I backtracked, and then as I was coming up towards the ditch, I walked a little farther down so I could come up around; as I came up on the ditch I was looking down on, it sort of sloped down, and I noticed something shiny. So I stopped and it was a little, it wasn't very level, so I braced myself, and I leaned down and I could just see a top part of, well, I just saw one part—I wasn't sure if it was a top part or whatever, so I reached down and I grabbed it, and then I stood up and I looked closer at it, I realized what I had picked up."

Did you count them? There are nineteen "I's" in that short verbal statement. It's easy to miss them, but they are an indicator of stress and, in this case, deception. The officer was found guilty of planting the bomb. If it is a written statement or, as in this case, a transcript you are evaluating, it's a good idea to use a highlighter and highlight the personal pronouns. It will help them stand out so you don't miss them. A lack of or overuse of "I" will be easier to spot. You should see the highlighting "sprinkled" through the statement, and that would be a good indication that the statement has passed the test.

You can also refer back to the statement by the man who stated his pregnant wife had shot herself with his work gun. There are twelve "I's" from line two through line six. That's a lot of seasoning!

How many personal pronoun I's (PPI) are in a sprinkle? Well, I'd say the following scale offers some guidelines for evaluating PPI for every 2–3 lines of a statement:

3–4: moderate signs of anxiety

5–7: extreme signs of anxiety

In written form, if the average is greater than one PPI per line in an area, it's moderate. Understand this is not an average over the entire statement, as the high use of PPI will usually discontinue after the deception. In a verbal statement, you need to listen for its overuse.

This is a good time to remind you that not everyone does everything. Remember that the stress associated with deception doesn't affect everyone and manifest itself in the same way each time. There are many signs of deception we've covered with more to come. These are good indicators that deception is present. But even good indicators of deception aren't perfect indicators, and you won't get all of them all the time.

Some statements may pass the length test but fail the tense test. Some may use the correct tense, but the article is wrong. Others may fail one of the other indicators of deception we are about to cover. Basically, the more we know about how people are deceptive, the less the chance someone will be able to sneak their deceit past us.

Chronological Order

Chronology in a statement is important. Whenever we truthfully tell a story to someone in written or verbal form, we recount events in the order they occurred. Anything that is out of chronological order in a statement should be questioned.

When I ask my students to write an account of their most recent day off, I know they will write it in chronological order. Not one student has ever produced a statement in which the events were in any other format. Therefore, when a statement appears out of chronological order, it should catch their attention immediately.

The following is a statement taken in regard to an armed robbery report. The transcribed version follows.

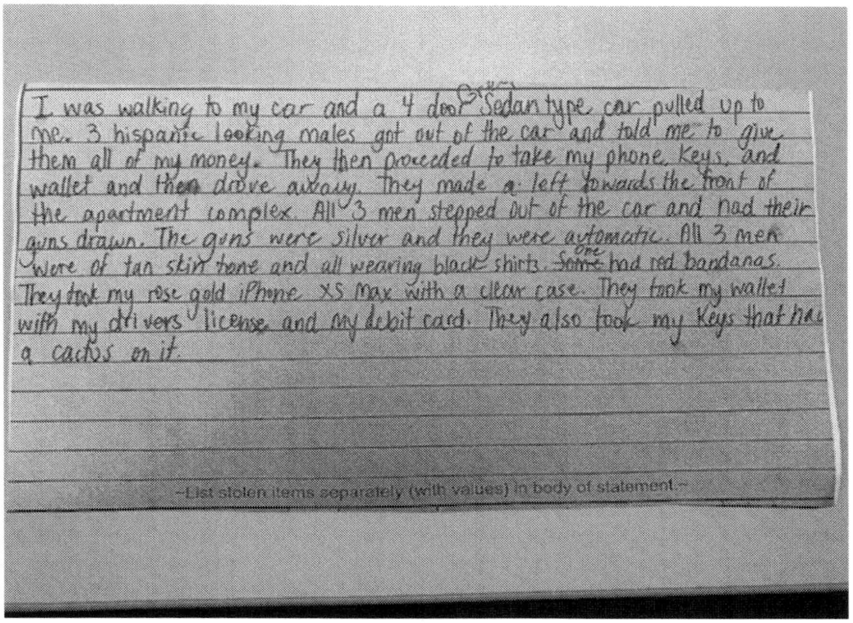

I was walking to my car and a 4 door Grey Sedan type car pulled up to me. 3 hispanic looking males got out of the car and told me to give them all of my money. They then proceeded to take my phone, keys, and wallet and then drove away. They made a left towards the front of the apartment complex. All 3 men stepped out of the car and had their guns drawn. The guns were silver and they were automatic. All 3 men were of tan skin tone and all wearing black shirts. ~~Some~~ One had red bandanas. They took my rose gold iPhone XS Max with a clear case. They took my wallet with my drivers license and my debit card. They also took my keys that had a cactus on it.

-List stolen items separately (with values) in body of statement.-

Transcript

I was walking to my car and a 4 door Grey Sedan type car pulled up to
me. 3 hispanic looking males got out of the car and told me to give
them all of my money. They then proceeded to take my phone, keys, and
wallet and then drove away. They made a left towards the front of
the apartment complex. All 3 men stepped out of the car and had their
guns drawn. The guns were silver and they were automatic. All 3 men
were of tan skin tone and all wearing black shirts. xx One had red bandanas.
They took my rose gold iPhone XS Max with a clear case. They took my wallet
with my drivers license and my debit card. They also took my keys that had
a cactus on it.

As you can read, the victim in this case writes, "All 3 men stepped out of the car and had their guns drawn." Providing that information is fine; however, the information is out of order. The next question should be "Why is this information out of chronological order?" Why would the subject forget to include this information where it belonged in the story? Chances are because the information is deceptive.

You see, there is an editing process people undertake when they tell their story, whether written or verbal. During that process, unimportant information is edited out and important information is included. In addition, as a victim statement, it also fails the 25-50-25 test from a previous lesson.

Consistency

An honest statement should be consistent regarding information known or alleged to have been known from the perspective of the writer. For instance, Casey Anthony stated she had "no idea" where her daughter Caylee was. Well, if she had dropped her off with the babysitter, shouldn't she have had some idea?

In 1994, Susan Smith reported to the police that her car, with her two sons still inside, had been carjacked by a black male. Yet when Smith later gave a statement to the media, she said, "I would like to say to whoever has my children that they please, I mean please, bring 'em home to us, where they belong." Well, if Smith had been carjacked by a black male, shouldn't she have been speaking directly to him? Many of us already know the tragic ending to that story: it was Susan Smith who had driven her car into a lake with her children still in the back seat.

Unique Information

Unique words or phrases in someone's written or verbal statement need to get your attention. By "unique words," I mean things that seem odd to include in a story. It may seem obvious when I point out some of these, but I can tell you that my friends in law enforcement miss them on a regular basis.

I'll start with the unique word "left." "Left" is unique because it's an indicator of stress or anxiety. It's a break from the norm. Generally, we don't write or tell people we left because we don't need to tell someone we *left* somewhere when we later say we *went* somewhere. The fact that we left is implied and doesn't need to be stated at all. For instance:

- "I left my house to go to the movies."
- "We left the party and went back home."

The norm is to state you went to the movies. Leaving home is implied. To be clear, I'm not stating here that this is an indicator of deception every time. But remember that the break from the norm can be an indicator. The person felt the need to tell us they left a location because subconsciously, there was anxiety there and leaving brought some relief. What's causing the tension? Grab your shovel and start digging—find out more about why they *left*.

The next word is "lights." Again, I've read many statements, including those by students in my training classes, and it's rare for anyone to mention lights in an open statement. When lights *are* mentioned without any prompting, it's usually an indicator of some sort of sexual activity. I once had a sex crimes detective in a class who said, "I see that in statements all the time." I assured him that property, auto theft, and homicide detectives don't see lights referenced in statements of the incidents they investigate. This applies to turning "on" or "off" lights or lights being "on" or "off" in locations. Remember, a statement (verbal or written) represents an edited version of what's important. If the person writes it or states it, it is important. Why are lights important? My students that write statements of their entire day, where they likely turned "on" and "off" many lights—but nobody includes it in their statements.

Basically, any time a subject describes activities in their statement that seem unimportant or unnecessary could be included. For example:

- Going to the bathroom
- Changing clothes
- Making phone calls

When unnecessary information enters an open statement, it's usually in place of other information the writer doesn't want to include. When the person goes into their memory, they know there's something significant that occurred at the time; knowing that it was significant, they subconsciously want to include it in their statement. However, they can't include this information without incriminating themselves, so they substitute it with other information. So the information itself is unimportant, but when included in a statement that should have already had insignificant details edited out of it, it signifies something deeper.

Below is an actual statement taken as part of a homicide investigation; the writer of the statement came home to find his grandfather, who had been shot and killed, on the sofa. See if you can spot the deception. I'll include a transcription of the statement following the written version.

> Left around 2:30-3 and went to go pick
> up my friend from school, the went got my other
> friend Devin then I took back my friend
> I got from school back home then went off
> with devin till around 9:45 went to my fri
> house to take him and his mom up for late
> dinner came back dropped my friend mom off
> went home saw all lights were off went
> inside saw things were gone saw him differen
> color went to check see whats wrong and
> then saw he was shot then called the cops
>
> ~List stolen items separately (with values) in body of statement.~

Transcript

> Left around 2:30–3 and went to go pick
> up my friend from school, the went got my other
> friend Devin then I took back my friend
> I got from school back home then went off
> with Devin till around 9:45 went to my friend
> house to take him and his mom up for late
> dinner came back droped my friend mom off
> went home saw all lights were off went
> inside saw things were gone saw him different
> color went to check see whats wrong and
> then saw he was shot then called the cops.

Let's go over this statement with the aspects of deception we've covered in mind. Remember that I didn't tell him how to write his statement; he decided how to write the story all on his own.

First, the statement begins at 2:30 p.m. He has gone into his memory and decided this is the farthest moment from the incident that still belongs to the incident. That's an unusual time to begin his story since he didn't find his grandfather until 10:30 p.m., don't you think? Couple that with beginning the statement and its use of the unique word "left." Remember, "left" indicates stress or anxiety experienced at the location he left. In this case, the house.

There is no personal pronoun "I" until two and a half lines into the statement. This indicates that he is distancing himself from his entire statement; he's not taking ownership of it. The victim, the writer's grandfather, doesn't come into the statement until line nine. When he does, he is introduced to the reader as "he." The social introduction is significant as it tells us about their relationship. The writer's grandfather got zero check marks on the social introduction chart. He didn't get a possession, a title, or a name. In his language, the writer is conveying this is not a good relationship.

These are all red flags and good places to put down our shovel to ask more questions. This writer later confessed to shooting and killing his grandfather. His statement offers many clues leading to that fact. You may have noticed I didn't mention that he wrote "all lights were off" in his statement. Interestingly, when he confessed, he stated his grandfather had sexually assaulted him when he was younger. I believed him.

Once again, the writer didn't provide any untruthful information in his statement. It was truthfully deceptive.

Here's a statement by someone whose house was on fire. Was the fire set intentionally, or was it ignited accidentally?

"I left my house right after breakfast to join my friends at the track for the day. I drove back to my house, made a few phone calls, then went out to dinner with Bruce Saunders. Bruce dropped me off at my house around 10:00. After I changed my clothes, I left the house to spend the night at my cousin Tom's house. Around midnight, we heard fire engines and got up to see what was going on."

Before reading through my observations, take a minute to write down your own observations.

There are several issues to address, working this statement from a statement analysis perspective. They are:

- The statement begins at breakfast, although the house wasn't found on fire until much later. Why? I think it's because that was when the writer decided he was going to set his house on fire.
- The word "left" in his comment about going to the track. This is an indicator of stress or anxiety. I believe that also references his decision to set his house on fire. Another arrow pointing us in the same direction.
- On line two, he wrote that he "made a few phone calls." This is an unnecessary activity in an open statement. Why was this information important? We know it was important, or it would have been edited out of the story. It's in place of other information the writer didn't want to include here.
- On line three, he wrote, "After I changed my clothes…" We have a word that spans time, "after," followed by an unnecessary activity, "changed my clothes." Again, this is

in place of information the writer doesn't want us to know. It represents a break from the norm for someone to write about changing their clothes in an open statement.

- Immediately following that is "I left the house." We have the flag word "left," and we no longer have the possessive "my" concerning the house. It had been "my house" three times previously, but no longer.

So, we have a flag with "after," with "changed my clothes," with "left," and with "the house." That's a lot of flags, and we should know exactly where to put our shovel down and dig. Once again, the statement doesn't contain anything we could say was untruthful. It was just truthfully deceptive.

We

"We" is the most important little word to focus on when conducting a statement analysis. "We" is important because it always indicates a good relationship: willing participants. Think about it. Would you ever use the word "we" concerning someone you didn't enjoy a good relationship with? Probably not. The same can be said for the pronouns "us" and "our," but I think "we" is the one used most often.

So why is it so important? Many times, law enforcement agencies around the country collect statements from people who claim they are victims of various incidents. In a truthful statement, it's highly unlikely that a victim would use the pronouns "we," "us," or "our" in describing their relationship with the suspect. Why? Because their relationship is not only *not* a healthy one, they're also being victimized by this person! You are also likely to see the same lack of these pronouns in close relationships, such as a marital relationship, if the person is describing being victimized.

These are very serious allegations, so law enforcement should take them very seriously. One of the things I always said when I was teaching Intro to CID is that we owe as much to the suspects in our cases as we do the victims. What I meant by that was that both the victim *and* the suspect deserve a fair, impartial, thorough investigation. Understand: doing a statement analysis doesn't replace that fair and thorough investigation. It is meant to enhance it by providing the investigator with insight on areas in the statement that need closer examination. I'm not suggesting that law enforcement close the case the minute they see this pronoun used in a victim statement. I'm suggesting that if some additional questions are asked, you will very likely discover what truly occurred.

If you find that a victim uses the words "we," "us," or "our" concerning themselves and the suspect, it's a strong indicator the contact between them was consensual. This is particularly true in cases involving an allegation of sexual battery. Because sexual battery is such a personal crime, victims often don't maintain positive relationships with a person who has committed those crimes against them. However, in telling their story, victims of these crimes will often reveal their true feelings for their alleged attackers without realizing it. They do this by the words they choose.

Some time ago, I was working in homicide when the quarterback from FSU, Jameis Winston, was accused of sexual battery by another student. The case was far from my jurisdiction, but my captain at the time had attended FSU and was very interested. My captain's interest made it interesting for me. So I researched on the internet and located the report and the victim's statement. Here it is:

CONTINUATION ☐
SUPPLEMENT ☐
STATEMENT ☑

TALLAHASSEE POLICE DEPARTMENT
OFFENSE REPORTING FORM
AGENCY NUMBER FL0370300

Page 1 of 1

Juvenile Involved ☐ Gang Related ☐
Domestic Related ☐ Firearm Involved ☐

Case/Incident Number: 12-032757

INCIDENT

Type of Crime or Incident on Original Report: Sexual Battery
Correct Crime or Incident: 32758
Location of Incident: Unk
Date of Original Report: 12-07-12
Date of This Report: 12-07-12
Victim's Name (Last, First, Middle), Arrestee or Business:
Property Recovered (If yes, enter value)

In the State of Florida/Leon County, ______ swears/affirms the following to be a true and accurate statement:

NARRATIVE

I was at Potbellys with Monique and Marcus, we all shared about 5 or 6 drinks. We were hanging out mostly with Marcus' friends. One of them gave me a shot. Monique left, I texted her to see if she had my ID and my room key, she said that she left all the stuff with me. Next thing I know I was in the back of a taxi with a random guy that I have never met. There was another person in the taxi. We went to an apartment, I dont know where it was. I kept telling him to stop but he took all my clothes off. He started having sex with me and then his roommate came in and told him to stop. He moved us to the bathroom "because the door locked" and I'm not 100% sure how everything in there happened. Afterwards I laid on his bed and he put my clothes on and we went outside and got on his scooter. He asked me where I lived and I told him Salley Hall. He dropped me off at Call & Stadium and then left.

ADMINISTRATIVE

I understand and know what I am doing. No promises/threats/coercion of any kind have been made to me in making this statement.
Signature

Sworn to and subscribed before me, the undersigned authority, this 7 day of Dec, 2012
Signature

Officer(s) Reporting/Dept. I.D. #: 1. Folli 671 — Date: 12-7-12
2.

Supervisor Approving/Dept. I.D. #: 1. 2. — Date

Case Status (Status must be indicated for all cases.) ☑ Open/Pending ☐ Closed
Case Disposition ☐ Unfounded ☐ Cleared by Arrest ☐ Cleared Exceptionally

PD 105
Revised 11/97

CENTRAL RECORDS

Now, I have no issue with the use of the word "we" in the initial part of the statement before the crime began. However, there should no longer be a "we" concerning the victim and the suspect during or after the description of sexual battery. The writer states, "He moved us to the bathroom…" and then continues, "…and we went outside and got on his scooter."

This language is not consistent with someone who had been sexually assaulted. I can't think of an instance where the use of the word "we" didn't indicate a good relationship with willing participants. A possible exception to this rule may be that of someone involved in a long-term abusive relationship, and the context of the usage would need to be considered. Some other issues, from a statement analysis perspective, in this statement are below.

Note the statement begins at Potbelly's. That was where the incident began. This is a victim statement from someone with significant involvement, so we can see how it measures against the 25-50-25 formula. The statement is seventeen lines. The main issue begins halfway through line eight. That's 50 percent into the statement.

As I said earlier, deceptive statements usually don't come close to 25-50-25. The main crime is roughly four lines long, and the content after the main issue is another four lines. So, roughly speaking, the statement is 50-25-25. That's not close.

Winston was never criminally charged as a result of the investigation. Objectivity in investigations does not discount the severity or criminality of any crime, including that of sexual battery. The primary question that an investigator should have concerning an allegation such as this instance is "Was the incident consensual or criminal?"

There was another incident that gained national attention: the allegation by Christine Blasey Ford of sexual battery by US Supreme Court nominee Brett Kavanaugh. You may remember there were televised senate hearings over this serious accusation. I was teaching on the day Ford testified before the committee and wasn't able to watch her testimony. However, I soon heard that Ford had written a statement detailing the incident that had occurred approximately thirty-six years prior. It was dated August 7, 2018. Once again, I searched the internet and located her statement; here it is, followed by a transcript:

One summer
~~While in~~ high school in ~~early~~ 80's,
I went to a small party in the
Montgomery County area. There were
4 ~~people~~ boys and a couple of girls.
At one point, I went up a small
stairwell to use the restroom. At
that time, I was pushed ~~by two~~
~~persons~~ into a bedroom and was
locked in the room and pushed onto a
bed. The boys were in the room. Brett laid on top of me
and tried to remove my clothes
while groping me. He held me
down and put his hand on
my mouth to stop me
from screaming for help. His
friend Mark was also in the room
and both were laughing. Mark
jumped on top of us 2 or 3
times. I tried to get out from
under unsuccessfully. Then Mark
jumped and we toppled
over. I managed to run out of
the room across to the bathroom
and lock the door. Once
I heard them go downstairs,
I ran out of the house and
went home.

Christine Blasey August 7, 2018

Transcript

Xx One high school summer in xx 80's
I went to a small party in the
Montgomery County area. There were
4 xx boys and a couple of girls.
At one point, I went up a small

> stairwell to use the restroom. At
> that time, I was pushed xx xx
> xx into a bedroom and was
> locked in the room and pushed onto a
> bed. The boys were in the room. Brett xx laid on top of me
> and tried to remove my clothes
> while groping me. He held me
> down and xx put his hand on
> my mouth xx to stop me xx
> from xx screaming for help. His
> friend Mark was also in the room
> and both were laughing. Mark
> jumped on top of us 2 or 3
> times. I tried to get out from
> under unsuccessfully. Then Mark
> jumped xx and we toppled
> over. I managed to run out of
> the room across to the bathroom
> and lock the door. Once xx
> I heard them go downstairs,
> I ran out of the house and
> went home.

I'm guessing you have already spotted the issues. Yes, Ford wrote, "Mark jumped on top of us 2 or 3 times" and "Then Mark jumped and we toppled over." Again, there is no "we" or "us" concerning a victim's relationship with someone committing a crime against them—particularly when the crime is as personal as a sexual battery. While Ford does far better with the 25-50-25 rule (this statement is roughly 23-57-20), when it comes to allegations of sexual battery in particular, the use of "we," "us," or "our" is difficult to overcome as it signals that good, positive relationship.

Here is my challenge to my students—can they go through their case files of statements and find a *suspect* statement (written or verbal) where the suspect uses the words "we" or "us" referring to themselves and their victim? No student has been able to do it, and I've had thousands of students who have investigated hundreds of thousands of cases. It simply doesn't occur because even suspects know their relationship with their victim wasn't a consensual one!

Now, many of you may be thinking, "Well, this is just a coincidence!" No, it's not. In one of my last months before I retired, there was an allegation of an attempted sexual battery made by a housekeeper against her supervisor. The area where I worked was very high profile, and allegations of this nature got a lot of attention. So, the question was immediately asked by my supervisor, "Did this really occur?" After I reviewed the victims statement, my answer was yes. Below is the actual statement by the victim in that case. A transcript will follow the written statement:

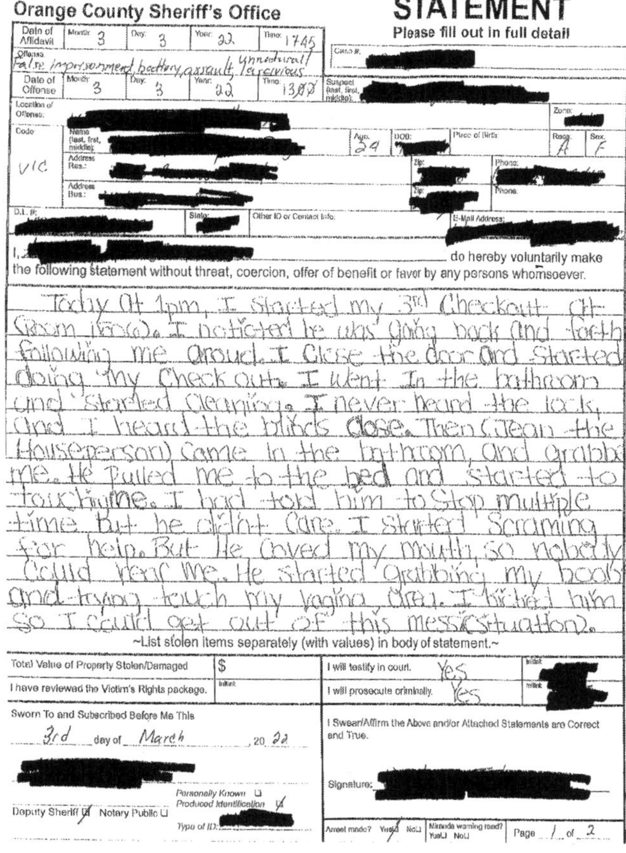

Orange County Sheriff's Office

STATEMENT

Please fill out in full detail

Date of Affidavit — Month: 3 Day: 3 Year: 22 Time: 1745

Case #:

Offense: False imprisonment, battery, assault, unnatural/lascivious

Date of Offense — Month: 3 Day: 3 Year: 22 Time: 1300

Suspect (last, first, middle):

Location of Offense: Zone:

Code: VIC — Name (last, first, middle): Age: 24 DOB: Place of Birth: Race: A Sex: F

Address Res.: Zip: Phone:

Address Bus.: Zip: Phone:

D.L. #: State: Other ID or Contact Info: E-Mail Address:

I, ______ do hereby voluntarily make the following statement without threat, coercion, offer of benefit or favor by any persons whomsoever.

Today At 1pm, I Started my 3rd Checkout At Room 1___. I noticed he was going back and forth following me aroud. I Close the door and Started doing my Check out. I went In the bathroom and started cleaning. I never heard the lock, And I heard the blinds close. Then (Jean the Houseperson) Came in the bathroom, and grabbe me. He Pulled me to the bed and started to touching me. I had told him to Stop multiple time but he didn't Care. I Started Scraming for help. But He Coved my mouth, so nobody Could hear me. He started grabbing my boobs and trying touch my vagina area. I kicked him so I could get out of this mess (situation).

~List stolen items separately (with values) in body of statement.~

Total Value of Property Stolen/Damaged: $

I have reviewed the Victim's Rights package. Initial:

I will testify in court. Yes Initial:

I will prosecute criminally. Yes Initial:

Sworn To and Subscribed Before Me This 3rd day of March, 20 22

Deputy Sheriff ☑ Notary Public ☐

Personally Known ☐

Produced Identification ☑

Type of ID:

I Swear/Affirm the Above and/or Attached Statements are Correct and True.

Signature:

Arrest made? Yes☑ No☐ Miranda warning read? Yes☐ No☐ Page 1 of 2

Orange County
Sheriff's Office

STATEMENT (Continuation)

Page 2 of 2 Case #: 22-8 14675 50

I Scream again, to get help. He told me, if you tell Manager or Anyone. I'm gonna Hurt you. Jean started touching me again. He didn't care and kept going. I kicked him one again to back him off. He told me again, if you tell Manager or anyone. I'm gonna find a way to hurt you. (DON'T TELL ANYONE) Jean said. I scream again and He finally left the room. After, I finished AM my checkout, He started following me around In my Stayover. He lock this time around In my Stayover and asked If I need help. I told him, No I don't need help. In every stayover he will Lock and ask if I need help. That's when I started speaking up. I told Cody first about what happened. I had to Speak up before this gone even wrost. I don't want this happen to anyone. What I experince, I don't want anyone else to doubt with.

Sworn To and Subscribed Before Me, This 3rd Day of March, 20 22 Deputy Sheriff ☐ Notary Public ☐ Personally Known ☐ Produced Identification ☑ Type: MI ID	I Swear/Affirm the Above and/or Attached Statements are Correct and True. Signature:

10-1181A (7/03) White - State Attorney's Office Yellow - Records Pink - Investigator

Transcript

Today at 1pm, I started my 3rd checkout at (room 150(a). I noticed he was going back and forth following me around. I close the door and started doing my check out. I went in the bathroom and started cleaning. I never heard the lock, and I heard the blinds close. Then (Jean the Houseperson) came in the bathroom, and grabbed

me. He pulled me to the bed and started to
touch me. I had told him to stop multiple
time but he didn't care. I started screaming
for help. But he coved my mouth, so nobody
could hear me. He started grabbing my boobs
and trying touch my vagina area. I kicked him
so I could get out of this mess (situation).
I scream again, to get help. He told me if
you tell manager or anyone, I'm gonna hurt you
Jean started touching me again. He didn't care
and kept going. I kicked him once again to back
him off. He told me again, if you tell manager
or anyone I'm gonna find a way to hurt you.
(DON'T TELL ANYONE) Jean said. I scream
again and He finally left the room. After I finished
my checkout, he started following me around In my
Stayover. He look this time around in my Stayover
and asked if I need help. I told him, No
I don't need help. In every Stayover he will
look and ask if I need help. That's when I
started speaking up. I told Cody first about
what happened. I had to speak up before
this gone even worst. I don't want this
happen to anyone. What I experience, I don't
want anyone else to doubt with.

This statement was written by an Asian female. If you recall, I previously stated truthful statements from victims who had significant involvement in an incident tend to be about a page to a page and a half. This is a victim statement and is someone with significant involvement.

Note that the statement is thirty-two lines, a page and a half, and the main issue begins on line seven. The main issue concludes on line twenty-two, so this statement is 23-48-29—almost exactly on the 25-50-25. There is no "we" or "us" as she describes the incident. It is always "I," "he," "him," or his name—and this is someone who was known to this particular victim. Yet there is no "we," "us," or "our" as she describes the event. This is very consistent with a truthful account of an incident such as this.

A Few Famous Cases and Baking the Cake

What do I mean by "baking the cake"? Well, if you assume what the person is telling you is true, or you consider the facts of an investigation, does it make sense? Using the person's statement or the facts as the "ingredients," can you bake the cake? If you can, that's a good sign. However, when someone is being deceptive or the facts don't seem to add up and leave something out of the "recipe," things don't quite fit together. You can't bake the cake.

Not all of these cases are solved cases, but we'll use the techniques of statement analysis and apply them to what are the known facts of these cases. Let's take a look at some examples.

Murder on a Sunday Morning

I'd like to revisit the documentary discussed in a previous lesson, *Murder on a Sunday Morning*. What I'd like to discuss isn't the focus of the documentary and isn't even something that is pointed out in the documentary. During the victim's husband's courtroom testimony, he recounts the incident where he and his wife were the victims of an armed robbery. In describing what occurred during the robbery/homicide, he states:

"All of a sudden, there was somebody in my wife's face and my face and said, 'Give me your pocketbook.' She first said, 'Oh,' like that, and she started to drop the pocketbook off her shoulder and her arm to give it to him."

He goes on to state, "After he told her to give him her pocketbook, he raised the pistol and shot her…"

One of the challenges I give to my students is that they have to assume he would offer the exact same information to them at the scene as he does on the stand. They get to ask him one question. What is the question?

The hint I give is that if they examine his testimony from a "baking the cake" perspective, they can solve it and win the challenge. Can you solve it without peeking below to see the answer?

As law enforcement, we work robberies on a fairly regular basis. Very few robberies escalate into homicides. Why? Because the purpose of the robbery isn't to commit a homicide; it's to gain money or property. Although committing a robbery with a firearm may result in a homicide, it's rare for that to actually occur. Most people cooperate with someone who is pointing a firearm at them, demanding money or property.

Here is the question—if the robbery was going so smoothly and his wife was being cooperative—as the man's statement leads us to believe—why did the suspect shoot her? Based on what he stated, I can't bake the cake.

Although investigating homicides doesn't require law enforcement to prove a motive, we nonetheless know there was one. But the man never states any motive for the suspect to shoot his wife. As we discussed in a previous lesson, he said two words that told us what he wasn't telling us.

Having all the facts keeps surprises from coming up later in the investigation. Much like I pointed out earlier with Roy Kronk's inability to be completely truthful with the detectives, it didn't change the fact that human remains had been found. The skills of statement analysis should be used to assist investigators in conducting complete, thorough investigations.

We use statement analysis to know where to put our shovel. We know the next questions to ask:

- "Why did the suspect shoot your wife if she was cooperating?"
- "What else did she say to the suspect?"
- "What else did your wife do when she was taking her purse off her shoulder?"

These questions now force the man to either lie or to come clean and tell the entire story, including the parts he initially chose to omit. He can no longer be truthfully deceptive.

Jussie Smollett Case

Now, I fully realize these are very simplified versions of the Smollett case and the JFK assassination. This is not an attempt to investigate these cases, only to examine some of the details as we know them by using and applying the skills we've discussed to both the verbal and non-verbal actions of the people involved. There are many, many more details. However, the details I presented are fairly well known and agreed upon.

On January 29, 2019, actor Jussie Smollett claimed he had been attacked in Chicago. Smollett stated that he had been walking down the sidewalk late at night when two white males wearing MAGA hats attacked him. The men yelled racial and homophobic slurs at him, poured bleach on him, and put a rope around his neck. The allegations of a serious hate crime caught the attention of many, including the media, politicians, and celebrities.

However, a closer look at the details revealed troubling inconsistencies. Among them:

- It had been negative sixteen degrees outside that night. How would anyone have even recognized Smollett, who would have certainly been dressed in warm clothing with much of his face covered?
- How would the attackers have even known who Smollett was? Smollett played a peripheral character on the show *Empire*. It's unlikely that racist white males were watching that particular show enough to be able to recognize the actor under the conditions present.
- Two white males wearing MAGA hats had been planning to attack a black male as part of a racist attack on the streets of Chicago in the middle of the night?
- Smollett alleged that he had been targeted in particular due to his race and/or sexual orientation. How would his attackers have known that Smollett had intended to leave his apartment at 2 a.m. to get a sandwich? What are the odds?

- Smollett left the rope around his neck until police arrived. Smollett also took officers down to the area where the attack occurred to show them a video camera.

Needless to say, the facts didn't add up, and Smollett was eventually charged with making a false police report. He was later convicted. You couldn't bake the cake based upon the recipe Smollett had provided. I was skeptical about the facts as they were being related, and I wasn't alone. I couldn't bake the cake based upon the recipe Smollett was providing.

JFK Assassination

Another case that can't bake a cake is the assassination of President John F. Kennedy. Like many others, I've read books and articles, watched movies and documentaries. The assassination of JFK has gripped the country—and even the world—since it occurred on November 22, 1963. Let's look at the case, as we would any other, from the standpoint of whether we can bake the cake based on what we know. I'm not going to attempt to analyze the thousands of details of the entire investigation here, only some of the actions of the main player, Lee Harvey Oswald.

As you are no doubt aware, the conclusions of many investigations, including the Warren Commission, have been that Lee Harvey Oswald acted alone to assassinate Kennedy. As that is the prevailing narrative concerning what occurred, we'll start from there.

We can all agree that Oswald shot his rifle from the fifth floor of the book depository where he worked. Prior to leaving the building, he was stopped and confronted by a Dallas police officer. After he was identified as an employee, the officer dismissed him, which means Oswald made it out of the building. Investigations concluded that Oswald took a bus and exited near his home.

According to a witness, Oswald was only at his house for a short time before he left again. While there, it's strongly suspected that Oswald armed himself with a handgun, the one he later used to kill a Dallas police officer. Obviously, a short time after Oswald left his house, he was stopped by another Dallas police officer. Okay so far?

Operating under the assumption that Oswald acted alone, here is the recipe of the cake:

- Oswald later killed the Dallas police officer but had made no attempt to kill the officer who had confronted him in the building. Why did Oswald believe the first officer was not a threat, but the second was? There were people present at both locations, so it wasn't due to the location or lack of witnesses.
- Oswald successfully planned and carried out the assassination of Kennedy by himself, complete with all the planning entailed, yet his getaway car was a city bus?
- Once he made it home, why would he have left so quickly? Police were not looking for Oswald. He was not yet even a suspect in the Kennedy assassination. Home is the ultimate place of safety and security, so why leave? And not only did Oswald leave, he also armed himself with the firearm he later used to shoot the officer, according to several investigations.
- Shortly after leaving his home, he came into contact with another Dallas police officer and shot him. Oswald would have known he was not yet a suspect in the shooting of the president; the scene was chaotic. So why shoot this officer? Shortly after, Oswald was arrested for the police officer's shooting. While in custody, Oswald stated he wanted representation and referred to himself as a "patsy" (Note: a "patsy" is someone easily deceived, a sucker). Two days later, on November 24, 1963, Oswald himself was assassinated as he was being led through the basement of Dallas Police Department Headquarters.

Well, there is some difficulty putting these pieces together, as some of them don't seem to quite fit. I can't bake the cake based on that recipe. However, if we view the details under the assumption that Oswald acted as part of a conspiracy, can they be explained? Let's see:

If Oswald had been part of a conspiracy, he had likely been told he was going to be transported out of the US, or at least from the area of the book depository. This would explain why he didn't attempt to harm the officer who confronted him in the building. The plan would have still been in play, and there would have been no reason to jeopardize everything by shooting the first officer.

A conspiracy would also explain why Oswald took a bus. If Oswald had been under the belief that he was going to be picked up by others involved, he wouldn't have needed to arrange any other transportation. This would have also been Oswald's first clue that the plan was not going as he had been led to believe—therefore causing a change in his demeanor, which we do see as Oswald began acting like a man in fear of his own safety *after* he left the book depository.

If he hadn't acted alone, Oswald's house would have been the least safe place he could have gone—it would be one of the first places his co-conspirators would look for him. This would explain why Oswald armed himself with a firearm and departed quickly.

When Oswald came into contact with another Dallas police officer, he would have recognized the plan was no longer as he had been led to believe—indeed, that he was a "patsy." He likely believed that he would be killed himself. Oswald had to know the officer wasn't seeking to arrest him for the shooting of the president. If the officer was going to attempt to arrest Oswald for the shooting of the president, don't you think he would have been prepared for an armed confrontation? Oswald likely believed the officer was going to kill him. This would explain his actions of shooting this officer in his then-panicked state.

While in custody, Oswald clearly wasn't going to remain silent. He declared he wanted an attorney and was indeed a patsy. This was a clear indicator that Oswald was part of a group. Had there been no group, there would have been no need for a patsy.

If there were co-conspirators involved, Oswald would have needed to be silenced. He was killed within days.

Unfortunately, none of Oswald's interviews while at the Dallas Police Department were preserved.

My point is that you would have to buy into many coincidences and improbabilities to believe in the single gunman theory. However, the pieces fit together pretty easily when operating under the assumption of a conspiracy. The statements and actions of Oswald make perfect sense when viewed from the perspective of someone who was part of a group, not of someone who acted alone.

I have trouble baking the cake when assuming that Oswald acted by himself under the lone gunman theory, but I have far less trouble with the verbal and non-verbal actions taken by Oswald when assuming he was acting with other conspirators.

JonBenet Ramsey Case

The last case I'd like to take a closer look at is the kidnapping/murder of JonBenet Ramsey. Many Americans are familiar with this story, as it is another case that caught the collective attention of our country. Everyone seems to have an opinion on it. For those not familiar with the case, here are some of the significant details.

On December 26, 1996, John and Patsy Ramsey awoke to find their six-year-old daughter, JonBenet, missing. They located a ransom note inside their residence. Also at home were John, Patsy, and JonBenet's nine-year-old brother, Burke, who all resided as a family.

While there are many aspects of this case, I'd like to focus on the ransom note. Let's use the tools for detecting deception we've covered and apply them here.

But first, why was the ransom so important? Well, aside from the girl's body, it was probably the most significant evidence in the investigation. If the ransom note was genuine, you have a kidnapping-turned-homicide. If the ransom note was a fraud, you have a kidnapping that's attempting to smokescreen a homicide. You can't have it both ways.

There are two major theories when it comes to this case: the family was involved, or intruders were involved. If the note was genuine, it would lean toward the intruder theory. If the note was a fake, it would lean toward the family theory. Simply put, an outside intruder would have no reason to attempt to "misdirect" the investigation. Only someone close to an investigation has an interest in misdirecting others.

Okay, so now that we have set the stage, here is a copy of the ransom note left at the residence:

Mr. Ramsey,

Listen carefully! We are a group of individuals that represent a small foreign faction. We respect your bussiness but not the country that it serves. At this time we have your daughter in our posession. She is safe and unharmed and if you want her to see 1997, you must follow our instructions to the letter.

You will withdraw $118,000.00 from your account. $100,000 will be in $100 bills and the remaining $18,000 in $20 bills. Make sure that you bring an adequate size attache to the bank. When you get home you will put the money in a brown paper bag. I will call you between 8 and 10 am tomorrow to instruct you on delivery. The delivery will be exhausting so I advise you to be rested. If we monitor you getting the money early, we might call you early to arrange an earlier delivery of the

money and hence a earlier ~~delivery~~ pick-up of your daughter.
Any deviation of my instructions will result in the immediate execution of your daughter. You will also be denied her remains for proper burial. The two gentlemen watching over your daugater do not particularly like you so I advise you not to provoke them. Speaking to anyone about your situation, such as Police, F.B.I., etc., will result in your daughter being beheaded. If we catch you talking to a stray dog, she dies. If you alert bank authorities, she dies. If the money is in any way marked or tampered with, she dies. You will be scanned for electronic devices and if any are found, she dies. You can try to deceive us but be warned that we are familier with Law enforcement countermeasures and tactics. You stand a 99% chance of killing your daughter if you try to out smart us. Follow our instructions

and you stand a 100% chance
of getting her back. You and
your family are under constant
scrutiny as well as the authorities.
Don't try to grow a brain
John. You are not the only
fat cat around so don't think
that killing will be difficult.
Don't underestimate us John.
Use that good southern common
sense of yours. It is up to
you now John!

Victory!

S.B.T.C

After reading the note, Patsy called 911 and, in a distraught voice, told the 911 operator that her daughter had been kidnapped and requested that police hurry to the residence. JonBenet was found dead in the family's basement by her father, John Ramsey, later that same day.

Now, let's go over the note. Hopefully, you have made your own observations. I'll start with page one:

Note that the kidnappers began by using the pronoun "we" and "our." This is consistent with someone writing on behalf of a group. However, before the end of page one, the writer switched to the pronoun "I." Was the writer no longer writing on behalf of a group? This is inconsistent. The writer also described the group as a "group of individuals." Isn't every group made up of individuals?

The beginning of the note states, "We respect your business, but not the country that it serves." So, according to the kidnappers, the motive of the kidnapping was political. However, this is inconsistent with what the writer stated later in the note. Are we to believe that kidnappers took a six-year-old in order to make a political statement? Also, John wasn't in politics. If the motive were political, wouldn't there have been far more attractive targets than JonBenet?

The kidnappers asked for $118,000. John Ramsey worked in the computer industry and was well paid. With people who had the assets of the Ramseys, doesn't that figure seem a little low? Last on page one, the writer uses the word "attaché" almost to convince us that he/they are foreign, as this word is associated more with European than American vocabulary.

The note goes into some delivery instructions and on the top of page two, it says, "and hence a earlier pick-up of your daughter." Now, "hence" isn't a commonly used word. It's used improperly because the word "and" isn't necessary. It should read: "hence, a earlier pick-up…" Just keep that in mind for a moment.

Page two details that the kidnappers were watching the Ramseys, and that if they alerted anyone, such as the police or the FBI, their daughter would be "beheaded." Again, this vocabulary, along with some of the other words used by the kidnappers, seems to want to convince the reader that they are indeed "foreign." But remember: I mentioned that Patsy called 911. Patsy made no mention of this to the 911 operator when she asked them to respond and "hurry!"

Well, according to the note, wouldn't that call have resulted in the kidnappers killing her daughter? This is not normal behavior. If your daughter were missing, and you read this note, would you even call 911? If you did, wouldn't you tell them that sending anyone to your house would result in your daughter's death, as the kidnappers would be watching? Patsy didn't even say anything about it.

On page three, the kidnappers get personal with John. So, is their motivation political or personal? Again, inconsistent. The note states, "Don't try to grow a brain John." When I first read the note, I thought that line sounded familiar. I researched a little and found that it's a line from the movie *Speed* when a character states, "Do not attempt to grow a brain." *Speed* was released in 1994.

Some other issues to consider are as follows:

A kidnapping with a ransom note is a highly unusual call for law enforcement. Why? Because the motive for a ransom is almost certainly money. People who have money (and who have been threatened with a ransom) will often not call the police and will call their attorney or a private investigator instead. You see, police are going to be focused on catching the kidnappers and won't take direction from a family. However, the family can call the shots if they have their attorney or PI involved. The family isn't nearly as interested in an arrest as they are getting their loved one back. I don't want to say police aren't interested in getting the person back safely, but police aren't going to serve as delivery boys for a bag full of money.

In the 911 call, I find it highly suspect that Patsy labels the incident a kidnapping. While I wasn't a 911 dispatcher, I've known a few and have listened to many 911 calls. It's rare for anyone to label the crime they're calling in, such as a "grand theft" or "suicide." A kidnapping is a conclusion, not a report. Why not say JonBenet was gone or had been taken?

It was later proven that the note was written using paper and a writing instrument from inside the residence. So are we to believe the kidnappers forgot to write their ransom note before going to the house?

Assuming the kidnapper(s) somehow lost control and killed JonBenet before even leaving the residence with her, why not still take her body? They could still have ransomed her, so why leave her behind?

In the 1997 memorial service held for JonBenet at their church, the Ramseys included the following passage: "Had there been no birth of Christ, there would be no hope of eternal life, and hence, no hope of ever being with our loved ones again." Not only do you have the same unusual word, "hence," being used here, but it is improperly used in the same way as the ransom note.

All of this leads me to conclude that the ransom note was a fake. Someone, or multiple people, were attempting to mislead the investigation. In 2006, John Karr was arrested in Thailand after he confessed to killing JonBenet. I recall the day the news broke. I commented to my wife that I knew he hadn't been involved, despite his confession. Although Karr was transported to Boulder, Colorado, charges against him were later dismissed, as it was determined that he wasn't involved.

No, when an attempt is made to mislead an investigation, it's invariably because the guilty party is close at hand. Someone who isn't close to the investigation has no need to mislead. In addition, not only would it be highly unlikely for the suspect(s) to leave the body behind, why then take the time to write out a ramson note?

Unfortunately, due to some missteps with the initial investigation, the homicide of JonBenet Ramsey will probably never be solved. There are too many potential issues with evidence to obtain a conviction.

What we *can* determine with reasonable certainty is that the note wasn't genuine and that JonBenet wasn't the victim of an attempted kidnapping. The rest is up to you.

Conclusion

Well, you made it! I hope you've enjoyed learning the skills involved in detecting deception. One of the best things about these skills is that you don't have to be a law enforcement officer to use them. I tell officers who take the training that they don't have to be working to use or hone these skills. You can implement them all the time, on duty or off duty.

Don't forget: the key ingredient to determining deception is that there has to be some form of jeopardy involved when providing the statement. Jeopardy causes stress, and stress is what causes the change(s) in verbal and non-verbal behavior. As I said, anxiety is usually a given with investigations, as the potential for incarceration looms if the person providing information is caught in a lie.

It has been my intention to take some of the mystery out of deceptive behavior, to make it easier to understand and to provide useful tools that anyone can use to determine the veracity of a statement. At the beginning of this journey into uncovering the truth, I asked you to think of a number between one and one hundred that would indicate how proficient you believed your ability at determining whether someone was being truthful or deceptive with you. I hope after reading this book, you feel more confident about that number. Continue to apply these principles, and they will work as well for you as they have for me.

I've always said that if something only works in a book or in some hypothetical situation and not in real life, why bother learning it? The same applies for these skills. Try utilizing them and see if reality confirms them—I'm certain it will. That's why I've given examples from events we are all familiar with and multiple real criminal cases, many with which I was personally involved.

These cases cover a variety of statements made by all types of people. There is no need for hypothetical examples when there are so many real examples. They cover those from the recent past and some from long ago. I chose this sampling intentionally to demonstrate the effectiveness of these skills. I didn't have to search for ones that confirmed the skills I've discussed in this book; they came across my desk. They were in the news on any given day, or I saw them on the internet. I'd be willing to bet they will for you as well.

Do you remember the number you wrote down at the beginning of this book? Take a look at it again. I hope you feel more confident in your ability to detect deception now than you did then. I've included a bibliography of resources that will help you continue to learn and enhance the skills covered in this book.

Good luck, and God bless!

Bibliography

Ariely, Dan. *The Honest Truth About Dishonesty: How We Lie to Everyone—Especially Ourselves.* New York, HarperCollins, 2012.

Ariely, Dan. *Predictably Irrational: The Hidden Forces That Shape Our Decisions.* New York, HarperCollins Press, 2008.

Carnegie, Dale. *How to Win Friends and Influence People.* Vermilion, 2019.

Craig, David. *Lie Detecting 101: A Comprehensive Course in Spotting Lies and Detecting Deceit.* Skyhorse, 2015.

Dawson, Roger. *Secrets of Power Negotiating: Inside Secrets from a Master Negotiator.* Career Press, 2001.

Ekman, Paul. *Telling Lies: Clues to Deceit in the Marketplace, Politics, and Marriage.* W. W. Norton, 2009.

Hartley, Gregory, and Maryann Karinch. *How to Spot a Liar: Why People Don't Tell the Truth...and How You Can Catch Them.* Career Press, 2005.

Houston, Philip, et al. *Spy the Lie: Former CIA Officers Teach You How to Detect Deception.* St. Martin's Press, 2012.

Karinch, Maryann. *Nothing But the Truth: Secrets from Top Intelligence Experts to Control Conversations and Get the Information You Need.* Weiser, 2015.

Lestrade, Jean-Xavier de, director. *Murder on a Sunday Morning.* 2001.

Lieberman, David J. *Never Be Lied to Again: How to Get the Truth in 5 Minutes or Less in Any Conversation or Situation.* St. Martin's Press, 1998.

Loeb, Daniel E. *Deception Detection: A Pocket Guide to Statement Analysis, Micro-expressions, Body Language, Interviews and Interrogations*. CreateSpace, 2013.

McClish, Mark. *I Know You Are Lying: Detecting Deception Through Statement Analysis.* The Marpa Group, 2001.

McClish, Mark. *Don't Be Deceived: The Definitive Book on Detecting Deception.* The Marpa Group, 2012.

McClish, Mark. "Statement Analysis® On-Demand Training." http://www.StatementAnalysis.com.

Navarro, Joe, and Marvin Karlins. *What Every BODY is Saying: An Ex-FBI Agent's Guide to Speed-Reading People.* William Morrow, 2008.

Navarro, Joe. *The Dictionary of Body Language: A Field Guide to Human Behavior.* William Morrow, 2018.

Nierenberg, Gerard I., and Henry H. Calero. *How to Read a Person Like a Book*. Pocket Books,1990.

Pease, Allan, and Barbara Pease. *The Definitive Book of Body Language: The Hidden Meaning Behind People's Gestures and Expressions*. Bantam Hardcover ed., Bantam, 2006.

Roche, Mike. *Face 2 Face: Observation, Interviewing and Rapport Building Skills: An Ex-Secret Service Agent's Guide.* Mike Roche, 2012.

Sapir, Avinoam. *Laboratory for Scientific Content Analysis.* http://www.lsiscan.com/.

Schafer, John R., and Joe Navarro. *Advanced Interviewing Techniques: Proven Strategies for Law Enforcement, Military, and Security Personnel*. Charles C. Thomas, 2004.

Tannen, Deborah. *That's Not What I Meant!: How Conversational Style Makes or Breaks Your Relations with Others*. Ballantine, 1991.

Tennant, Don, et al. *Get the Truth: Former CIA Officers Teach You How to Persuade Anyone to Tell All*. St. Martin's, 2016.

Voss, Chris, and Tahl Raz. *Never Split the Difference: Negotiating As If Your Life Depended On It*. HarperCollins, 2016.

Wezowski, Kasia, and Patryk Wezowski. *Without Saying a Word: Master the Science of Body Language and Maximize Your Success*. AMACOM, 2018.

Williams, James W. *How to Read People Like a Book: A Guide to Speed-Reading People, Understand Body Language and Emotions, Decode Intentions, and Connect Effortlessly*. James W. Williams, 2020.

Wilson, Glenn D. *Body Language: A Practical Guide*. Icon Books, 2016.

About the Author

For over 30 years in his career in law enforcement, Mike Ruggiero has used the skills he provides in this book to work and supervise Major Crimes from Sex Crimes to Internal Affairs, to Homicide.

During that time, Mike developed a unique skillset to help him determine when and how people were being forthcoming, were omitting, or were fabricating information.

Mike worked to receive his BA in Criminal Justice and is a frequent lecturer on the topics of Detecting Deception as well as Interview and Interrogation.

Mike breaks down the topics and makes it easy for anyone to learn these valuable skills.

www.PTIUncovertheTruth.com

Made in the USA
Middletown, DE
14 February 2025

71183323R00079